A TASTE OF THE

MARGARET River

PETER FORRESTAL

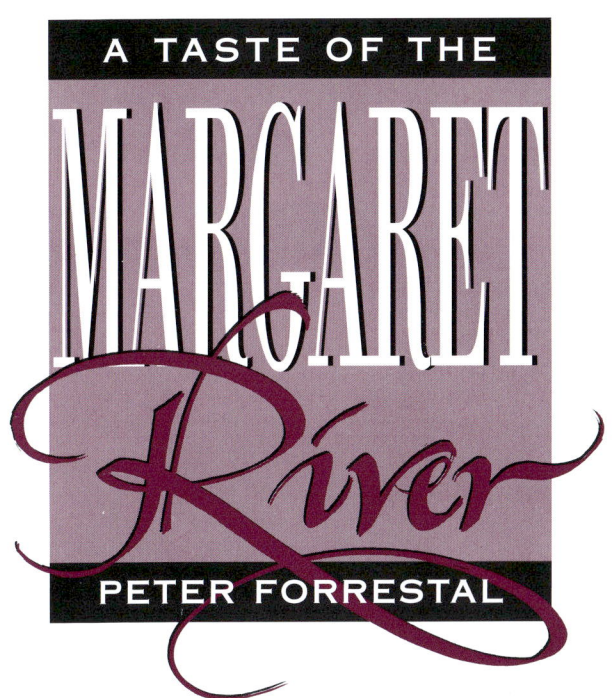

OCEAN GLIMPSES

First published in Australia 1995 by
Ocean Glimpses
1 Cobb Street
Scarborough 6019

National Library of Australia
Cataloguing-in-Publication data

      Forrestal, Peter
      A taste of the Margaret River: a guide to the wines,
      wineries and food of the region.

      ISBN 0 646 23384 X

      1. Wineries - Western Australia - Margaret River Region.
      2. Wine and wine making - Western Australia - Margaret River
         Region.
      3. Restaurants - Western Australia - Margaret River Region.
      4. Margaret River Region (W.A.) - Description and travel.
      I. Title. (Series: Wines of Western Australia).

338.766320099412

Cover painting: *Margaret Moonlight* by George Haynes.
Used by permission of the artist.

Designed by Robyn Mundy, Mundy Design.
Maps by Paul Mitchener.
Typeset in Berkeley Book 10.5 pt.
Produced by Ocean Glimpses.
Printed by Scott Four Colour Print, Perth, Western Australia.

For Bill and Sandra Pannell,
pioneers of the Margaret River wine industry,
and good friends.

Many thanks to the vignerons of Margaret River for the time they gave and the support, hospitality and friendship that they extended to me during the writing of this book.

My sincere thanks also to Pauline McLeod and the Augusta Margaret River Tourist Bureau and to the Western Australian Tourism Commission.

Thanks for their inestimable help to Robyn Mundy, Debbie Miller, Jane Crawford and Athena Georgiou.

Many of the wines reviewed in this book were tasted with two panels which I ran for the wine column of the *West Australian*. I am grateful for being able to share the good company and knowledge of Nevil Phillips (Chairman), Brian Fletcher and Lexie Thompson; Stephen Leslie (Chairman), Marg Johnson, Bill Pannell and Louis Papaelis. Judi Cullam, Bill Crapsley, David Gregg and Lisa Jones also joined us when possible.

I have learnt much over the years from the members of the Wine Group and Oenophiles as well as Graham Greenacre and the Liberty Liquors tasting panel and Kevin Lukey and the Scarborough Liquor Centre tasting panel. My taste buds were first tantalised by Jon Cook with whom I have enjoyed many memorable bottles. Two great enthusiasts who have played significant roles in my love affair with wine have been JJ and Steph Toole.

Special thanks to Elaine, for her support and forbearance and to Munch, the wonder dog, and the little Bopper who shared many hours around the computer while I worked on the manuscript.

Contents

A Guide to the Wineries

NOTE: The maps of the wineries can be found at the back of the Guide on pages 152 - 155.

FORRESTAL FAVOURITES: In most of the winery entries, one or more wines is described under this heading. It is unlikely that you will still be able to buy the particular wines mentioned here. They are included to give an indication of the style of my favourite wines from the vineyard.

About the wineries

WHILE every effort has been made to ensure that details were accurate when the book went to print, some changes may occur. The cost of individual wines is included to show the general level of prices at each winery and to indicate the relative cost of each of the wines.

All wineries give a discount on whole case (one dozen) purchases and most are willing to freight wine to any address in Australia. Mailing lists are operated by all of the region's wineries to keep in touch with their most regular customers. Being on a mailing list gives you preferential access to new releases at better than cellar door prices. Some wineries offer special wines to cellar door and mail order customers only.

The maps

The map on page 152 shows the most important roads for travellers wanting to get to know the area and its wineries. Familiarity with this map will give you a good understanding of the parameters of the region. It is on or off these roads that almost all of the wineries are found.

Only roads which are significant for reaching wineries are included on these maps.

Bussell Highway and Wallcliffe Road are reasonably wide and straight: a rarity in the area. Caves Road has been widened in places but is often quite narrow and bendy. The other major roads are either narrow or very narrow and have many bends or blind corners. Therefore caution needs to be exercised when travelling about the region.

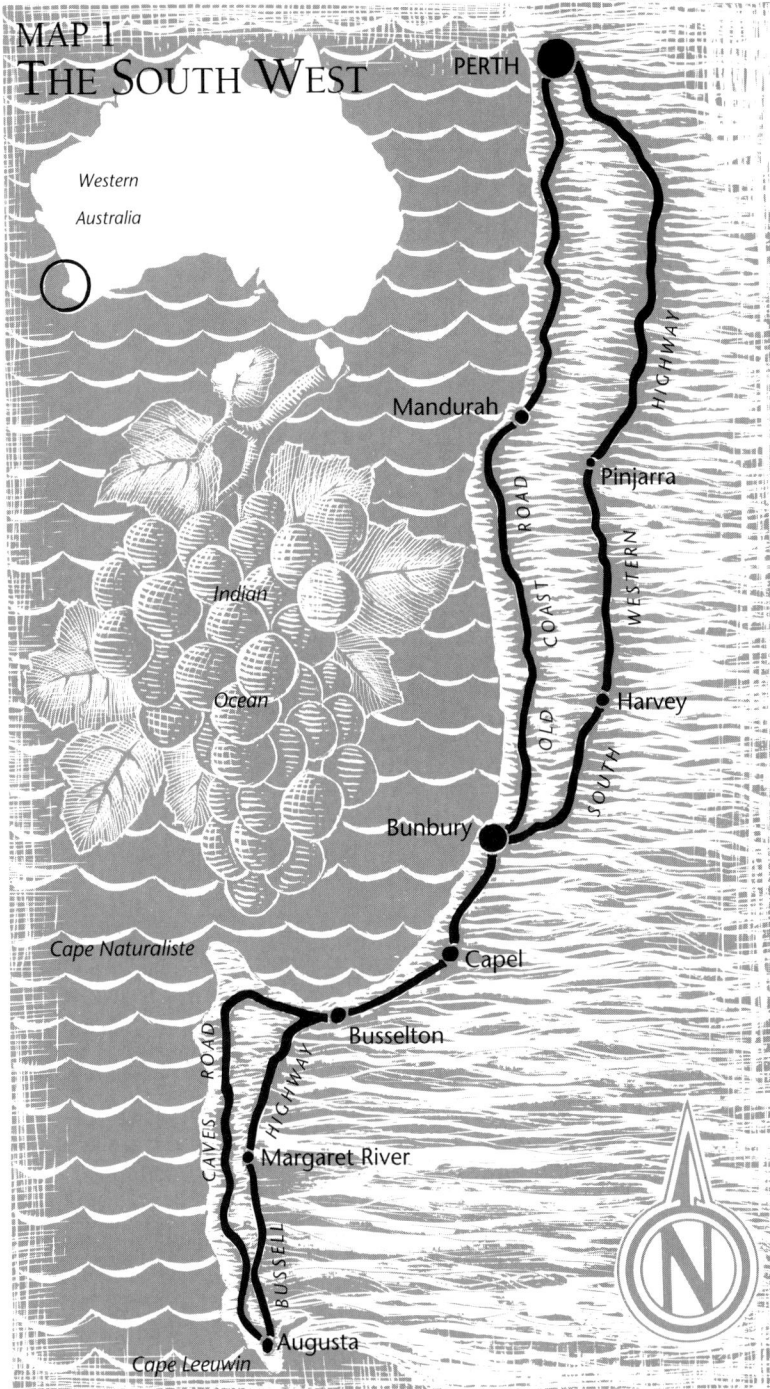

MAP 1
THE SOUTH WEST

Western
Australia

Indian

Ocean

Cape Naturaliste

Cape Leeuwin

PERTH

Mandurah

Pinjarra

Harvey

Bunbury

Capel

Busselton

Margaret River

Augusta

OLD COAST ROAD

WESTERN HIGHWAY

SOUTH

CAVES ROAD

HIGHWAY

BUSSELL

Getting there

By car

Distance: 290 kilometres. Travelling time about three and a quarter to three and a half hours.

Take the Kwinana Freeway until its finish, and then follow the signs for Rockingham, Mandurah and Bunbury by turning right into Thomas Road, then left into Rockingham Road. Follow the signs for Mandurah and Bunbury by turning left into Ennis Road which becomes Fremantle Road. Continue on and bypass Mandurah connecting with the Old Coast Road to Bunbury.

To bypass Bunbury, follow the signs to Capel and Busselton and connect with Bussell Highway. Turn left at the traffic lights in Busselton and about eight kilometres further on, go left following the Bussell Highway at the Vasse Turn-off to Margaret River or go straight ahead and follow Caves Road to Dunsborough and Yallingup.

By bus

Westrail Coach Services   *Reservations 13 2232*
Ex Perth: Mon & Wed 4pm; Tues & Thurs 12.20pm;
Fri 4.45pm; Sun 3.30pm.
Leaves the East Perth Railway Terminal, Summers Street.
Ex Margaret River: Mon-Thurs 8.40am; Fri and Sat. 8.10am.
Leaves the Travel Centre, opposite the Settlers Tavern.
Cost $24.50 one way.

South West Coachlines   *Reservations (09) 324 2333*
Ex Perth: 1.30pm daily from the Wellington Street Bus Terminal.
Ex Margaret River: from the Tourist Bureau, Mon-Sat 7am. and Mon-Fri 4.20pm.
Cost $23 one way.

Chartered aircraft

Royal Aero Club of WA (09) 332 7722

The club has more than 50 planes, both single and twin engine, that can accommodate a party of any size. Simply ring for a quote or a booking.

Skyworx (09) 246 2156

Paul and Cathy Hewett arrange scenic flights and air tours of the South West caves and wineries. Tours for a minimum of two includes pick up and return to hotel, lunch, a drive through Boranup Forest, exploration of the Lake Cave and visits to several wineries.

Tours

Luxury private tours of the wineries of the Margaret River region are organised by Brian Bedwell's Business Travel. These guided tours are intended for small groups, generally, of two to six people wanting to visit Margaret River in a day. They can be arranged with twenty four hours notice and include limousine transport to and from city hotels, twin engine flight to Busselton, limousine travel to selected wineries and a sumptuous lunch with top wines. Tours can be tailored to individual interests. Expensive.
Phone Brian Bedwell (09) 382 4255

Wine Tours of WA run regular one and two day tours of the Margaret River wineries using air conditioned coaches. The weekender includes lunch on both days, dinner on Saturday evening, accommodation, a continental breakfast, and visits to seven wineries (although some may be outside the Margaret River region) for $175. The one day trip includes lunch, a light dinner and visits to four wineries for $60. Good value.
Contact Bruce Cohen (09) 321 0870.

ABBEY VALE

ABBEY Vale owners, Bill and Pam McKay, have had an incredibly varied and adventurous life. They left Northern Ireland in their early twenties so that Bill could work as an engineer in Uganda for the British Foreign Office. He established a private electronics business and after five years, he moved to Vancouver and later to Perth. At the age of forty, his electronics firm was taken over. Bill then undertook five years of full-time study to qualify as a clinical psychologist.

The Abbey Vale property was purchased in 1975 as an investment. When their son, Kevin, became interested in viticulture after helping to plant Amberley Estate, the McKays established their vineyard in 1985 and 1986. All the fruit from the first few crops was sold to Houghton under long term contract and eventually they marketed a small amount under their own label. At this point, Bill and Pam decided that they would become involved in Abbey Vale and began yet another career.

Not content with this, and believing that Abbey Vale would need to do more than sell wine to survive, Bill enrolled in a summer course in brewing at the University of Davis, Sacramento. On his return, he established the Moonshine Brewery at Abbey Vale which produces up to 3,000 litres of beer per week.

The vineyard came to prominence when the McKays took the bold step of hosting an alfresco Festival of Perth concert with the Budapest Symphony at the vineyard in 1994. The concert is destined to become an established event on the Margaret River calendar and, in 1995, featured the Odessa Philharmonic Orchestra.

The Abbey Vale wines are well-made, flavoursome and approachable. Several will appeal to those who enjoy some sweetness.

FORRESTAL FAVOURITES

1994 Verdelho
A powerful, fruity white that is clean and fresh with strong, ripe passionfruit characters and a long dry finish.

1992 Sauvignon Blanc
A restrained style with a light, grassy nose and a hint of oak. It is clean, fresh and soft with some sweetness filling out the mid-palate and being obvious on the finish.

1991 Semillon
The vineyard's most serious wine, matured in new French oak for eight months, it has a pungent, toasty oak nose, good intensity of flavour on the mid-palate, is tightly structured and has a long, dry woody finish.

Wildwood Road, Yallingup.
(Take Wildwood Road off Bussell
Highway, travel 11km to Abbey
Vale entrance.)

Postal address
Post Office YALLINGUP 6282

Phone (097) 552 277
Fax   (097) 552 286

Hours of opening
10.30 am to 5pm daily

Cafe
Open from 10.30 am to 5pm daily
for lunch, morning and afternoon
teas.

Specialities
Moonshine Beer: Moonshine Bitter,
Moonshine Pale; Tee shirts

Owners
Bill and Pam McKay

General Manager
Carmel Gerrans

Viticulturist
Kevin McKay

Winemaker
Dorham Mann

Established
1986

Production
300 tonnes
4 200 cases (1993)
6 500 cases (1994)

Area planted
25.5 ha.

Varieties planted
Chardonnay	1.0 ha.
Chenin Blanc	1.0 ha.
Sauvignon Blanc	1.0 ha.
Semillon	8.0 ha.
Verdelho	5.0 ha.
Cabernet Sauvignon	5.0 ha.
Merlot	4.0 ha.
Shiraz	0.5 ha.

Wines produced

Abbey Vale Festival White	*$13*

1993 semillon 60%, sauvignon blanc 40%.
1994 semillon 70%, verdelho 15%, sauvignon blanc 15%.
Has some residual sugar and therefore finishes quite sweet.

Abbey Vale Sauvignon Blanc	*$15*
Abbey Vale Semillon	*$18*
Abbey Vale Sunburst Verdelho	*$12*

A late picked, and therefore, sweet verdelho.

Abbey Vale Verdelho	*$14*
Abbey Vale Cabernet Sauvignon	*$16*

AMBERLEY

SOUTH African, Albert Haak, knew enough about the viticultural potential of Margaret River to respond positively to his brother-in-law, Mark Turner's suggestion that they become jointly involved in the wine industry in that region. Albert and his wife Bridget emigrated from South Africa in late 1985 and searched for suitable land. When they found the perfect block and it was not for sale, Albert approached its owner, dentist Michael Sturgeon. As it turned out, he was keen to utilise the block and happily sold it to a holding company in return for a share in the venture.

The first vines were planted in 1986 and the first crop from the 1989 vintage was sold off to other producers. The winery was built in time for the following vintage.

Albert Haak had decided to plant substantial quantities of chenin blanc because of the variety's success in South Africa. The Amberley Chenin has become the winery's flagship with more than 13,000 cases sold within six months of its release. It is an easy-drinking commercial wine which is clean, pleasant and fruity with ripe flavours and a sweet finish.

Amberley was the first Margaret River producer to state its overt, commercial intentions and to price its wines so that some of them could be sold (in the early 90s) under $10. Because of its anticipated, eventual crush, Amberley needed to price its biggest selling wines so that they could be moved easily.

Amberley has been spectacularly successful and the current demand for its wines cannot be met from estate grown grapes. Fortunately, it has been able to secure long term contracts with local growers. The yield from the estate is expected to rise from 270 to 350 tonnes due to the increased maturity of the vines and the impact of experiments which have matched each variety and its soils with trellising and pruning methods.

Following a difference of opinion about future directions for the winery, Albert Haak, Amberley's driving force during its formative years, decided to leave to work as a freelance consultant specialising in vineyard development

FORRESTAL FAVOURITE

1993 Chardonnay
A soft and flavoursome white with delicate peach, tropical fruit and toasty oak aromas. The 1994 is a much better wine and was awarded four and a half stars as top chardonnay in the **Winestate** *tasting of Western Australian wines in December 1994.*

Owners

A private company owned by Mark and Sheryl-Lynn Turner, John Brunner, Michael Sturgeon, Peter Hugo, Corrado and Beverley Minutillo, Brian Steggall, Martin Haak, Nick Fisher, Yvonne Wallis, Keith and Sandra Yelverton and Philip Nicholls.

Chief Executive/Winemaker

Eddie Price

Viticulturist

Brian Williamson

Established

1986

Production

270 tonnes
22,000 cases (1993)
30,000 cases (1994)

Area planted

31.51 ha.

Varieties planted

| Chardonnay | 3.17 ha. |
| Chenin Blanc | 5.89 ha. |

Thornton Road, Yallingup.
(From Bussell Highway travel down Wildwood Road for just over 12km, turn left into Thornton Road. The entrance is about 600 metres from the corner.
Off Caves Road, take Wildwood Road for about 6 km to Thornton Road.)

Postal address
PO Box 319
BUSSELTON 6280

Phone (097) 552 288
Fax (097) 552 171

Hours of opening
10am to 4.30pm daily

Cafe
10am to 4.30pm daily

Specialities
Tee shirts, art works, ceramics, pottery.

Sauvignon Blanc	4.64 ha.
Semillon	7.85 ha.
Cabernet Franc	1.08 ha.
Cabernet Sauvignon	4.69 ha.
Merlot	3.14 ha.
Shiraz	1.05 ha.

Wines produced

Amberley Estate Chardonnay	$19
Amberley Estate Chenin Chenin blanc 70%, sauvignon blanc 30%.	$12
Amberley Estate Margaret River Classic Semillon 70%, chardonnay 20%, sauvignon blanc 10%.	$16
Amberley Estate Sauvignon Blanc	$16
Amberley Estate Sauvignon Blanc/Semillon	$17
Amberley Estate Semillon	$17
Amberley Estate Semillon/Sauvignon Blanc	$15
Amberley Estate Nouveau	$12
Amberley Estate Cabernet Merlot	$16

ARLEWOOD

BOTH John and Liz Wojturski started their working lives as Maths teachers. Liz has been a deputy principal since 1978, firstly at Mount Barker and, since 1984, at the nearby Busselton Senior High School. John taught part time in 1988 and 1989 while he planted the vineyard, took leave without pay during 1993 and 1994 and resigned to work full time at Arlewood from the beginning of 1995.

While at Mount Barker, the Wojturskis had a farm in the Porongurups on which they planted a commercial crop of flowers. After moving to Busselton, they looked for a similar place and, in June 1984, found a property in the Willyabrup Valley. This had been partially cleared by neighbour, Brian Devitt, for its Italian owner who had wanted to plant a vineyard. He was tracked down in Bolivia and accepted an offer to sell to the Wojturskis.

John and Liz took long service leave in 1986 and travelled to France where they fell in love with the lifestyle and, in particular, the town of Arles in Provence: something which Liz remembered when they were struggling to think of a suitable name for the vineyard.

Since then, there has been plenty of hard work: making mud bricks and helping build their house,

establishing a plant nursery in 1987, planting the vineyard in 1988 and looking after the vines ever since. The first vintage took place in 1991, the attractive, Mediterranean style cellar door outlet was completed in 1993 and the vineyard size is currently being doubled with plantings of sauvignon blanc, some merlot and shiraz and a small amount of cabernet franc.

At present, the Arlewood Estate Cabernet Sauvignon and the Semillon are made from estate grown grapes and the other wines are produced with purchased fruit.

FORRESTAL FAVOURITES

1992 Semillon
This wine from the vineyard's second crop has a floral, lifted bouquet with hints of citrus, grassiness and spicy oak while the palate is soft, full-flavoured and balanced with good fruit oak integration and a pleasant aftertaste.

1991 Cabernet Sauvignon
An approachable red with attractive minty, berry and charry oak characters. It is supple and full flavoured though a touch lean on the mid palate because it is from young vines. Expect future vintages to show more generosity.

Owners
John and Liz Wojturski

Winemaker
Mike and Jan Davies

Established
1988

Production
25 tonnes
800 cases (1993)
1200 cases (1994)

Acreage planted
2.4 ha.

Varieties planted
Cabernet Sauvignon   1.0 ha.
Semillon   1.4 ha.

Harmans South Road, Willyabrup.
(From Caves Road, turn into
Harman's Road South and follow it
for just over 3km.
From Bussell Highway, follow
Harmans Mill Road and turn left
into Harmans Road South for about
1km. The entrance is between
Ashbrook and Vasse Felix and the
cellar door is more than a kilometre
down a windy bush track.)

Postal address
PO Box 139
COWARAMUP 6284

Phone (097) 556 267
Fax   (097) 556 267

Hours of opening
11am to 5pm daily

Specialities
Tee-shirts, art exhibitions in the
tasting room.

ARLEWOOD

Margaret River
CABERNET SAUVIGNON
1991

PRODUCE OF AUSTRALIA   750ml

Wines produced

Arlewood Estate Cabernet Sauvignon	*$15*
Arlewood Estate Semillon	*$14*
Arlewood Estate White *Semillon 50%, sauvignon blanc 30%, verdelho 20%.*	*$12*
Arlewood Estate Liaison *A sweet wine made from muscat à petit grains produced outside the* *Margaret River region.*	*$10*
Arlewood Estate Port *Made from cabernet sauvignon.*	*$15*

ASHBROOK

HOLIDAYS on family land near Dunsborough, instilled a love of the region in the Devitt family. A range of influences aroused Tony Devitt's interest in the wine industry: studying with Dr John Gladstones at university; playing cricket with Tony Mann and hence coming to know his father, Houghton winemaker, Jack Mann, and working with Dorham Mann at the Agriculture Department.

When Dorham left to become winemaker at Sandalford in 1973, Tony Devitt took over his job as viticultural adviser and was sent by the Department to Roseworthy College to study winemaking. During holidays, he visited Margaret River looking for land for a vineyard. After a long search, he managed to find the perfect place.

When Tony finished his winemaking course and Brian returned from eighteen months in England, the two brothers commuted from Perth to establish the vineyard in 1976. After a few years, Brian Devitt was able to get a job teaching in Busselton and so live on the property.

There followed a decade of part-time work on the vineyard, until Brian resigned from teaching and took on the job of managing the estate full time. Tony Devitt has managed to combine his interest in the family winery with his day job as Manager of Horticultural Industries with the Department of Agriculture which gives him responsibility for viticulture within the state.

Although many believe that riesling is not suited to the area, the Devitts have refused to accept this viewpoint and produce the region's best example of the variety. The Gold Label Riesling is made only from free run juices and is fermented dry while the Black Label is a fruity white which includes some pressings and is left with a touch of residual sugar. The former has distinct citrusy, limey varietal character, is always spotlessly clean and well made with good flavour and crisp acidity.

Both their Semillon and Verdelho are unwooded, show excellent varietal and regional character and are among the best examples of these wines from the region.

FORRESTAL FAVOURITE

1993 Semillon

Arguably the best example of this variety from Ashbrook to date, it has a beautifully perfumed nose, attractive grassy characters and a crisp, dry finish. It is a delicious, fresh, clean wine with very good regional and varietal definition, excellent balance and the potential to make summer lunches even more memorable.

Owners
The Devitt Family

Chief Executive
Brian Devitt

Winemakers
Tony and Brian Devitt

Established
1976

Production
130 tonnes
6,000 cases (1993) 70 tonnes
(because of a massive hailstorm)
11,000 cases (1994)

Area planted
11.3 ha.

Varieties planted

Cabernet Franc	0.1 ha.
Cabernet Sauvignon	1.8 ha.
Merlot	0.1 ha.
Riesling	1.6 ha.
Chardonnay	3.4 ha.
Sauvignon Blanc	0.4 ha.
Semillon	2.8 ha.
Verdelho	2.2 ha.

Harmans Road South, Willyabrup
(From Caves Road, turn into
Harmans Road South and follow it
for just under 4 km.
From Bussell Highway, follow
Harmans Mill Road and turn left
into Harmans Road South.)

Postal address
PO Box 263
WEST PERTH 6005

Winery
Phone　　(097) 556 262
Fax　　　(097) 556 290

Perth Office
Phone　　(09) 364 1608
Fax　　　(09) 457 5535

Hours of opening
11am to 5pm daily

Wines produced

Ashbrook Chardonnay	$19
Ashbrook Black Label Rhine Riesling	$13
Ashbrook Gold Label Rhine Riesling	$13
Ashbrook Semillon	$13
Ashbrook Semillon Reserve	$15
Ashbrook Sauvignon Blanc	$16
Ashbrook Verdelho	$15
Ashbrook Cabernet Sauvignon	$19

BROOKLAND VALLEY

THE energy of the Jones family and their commitment to excellence is apparent to even the casual visitor who drives past the immaculately tended vines to taste wine or dine at Flutes Cafe with its idyllic setting on the dammed waters of the Willyabrup Brook.

For many years, the Jones family had agricultural properties and had bought a Margaret River dairy farm in 1983 as a weekend retreat. They considered becoming involved in the cheese industry but David Gregg, then owner of Vasse Felix, persuade them that the property was particularly suited to viticulture.

Working as a consultant had made Malcolm Jones aware of the importance of having the best possible advice in undertaking any venture. From the outset, the Joneses involved Australia's foremost winemaking consultancy, Oenotec, in planning the new vineyard. Therefore Brian Croser and Tony Jordan, were involved in extensive planning and analysis so that the vineyard could be designed and developed incorporating new technology. Consequently, the vines were closely planted to control vigour, high vertical trellising was used to give greater fruit exposure, a computer operated irrigation

system was set up to operate in the vineyard, organic fertilisers and organic sprays have been used as much as possible and extensive windbreaks have been planted to minimise wind damage.

The wines from Brookland Valley have improved with each vintage. The Sauvignon Blanc is a fresh, fruity style in the tropical fruit rather than grassy, herbaceous spectrum and is made to be drunk young. The Chardonnay is a fresh fruit driven style highlighting ripe peach, melon and toasty oak flavours which gains additional complexity with time in the bottle.

The premium red blend is approachable on release but will age in the short to medium term. The cabernet franc tends to give a fresh, uplifted character, the merlot a suppleness and roundness on the mid palate and the cabernet sauvignon a depth of sweet berry flavour.

FORRESTAL FAVOURITE

1994 Sauvignon Blanc
A wine which will brighten up even the sunniest day was the gold medal winner at the 1994 Sheraton Awards; it is simply delicious. It is a delicate, supple wine with distinct varietal character in the gooseberry, passion-fruit and tropical fruit spectrum, has intensity of flavour and a long, soft finish.

Owners
Malcolm and Dee Jones

Chief Executive
Malcolm Jones

Winemaker
Gary Baldwin
(Oenotech Consulting Services)

Viticulturist
Malcolm Jones

Established
1984

Production
220 tonnes
5,500 cases (1993)
7,500 cases (1994)

Area planted
20 ha.

Varieties planted

Chardonnay	8.5 ha.
Sauvignon Blanc	2.0 ha.
Cabernet Franc	1.5 ha.
Cabernet Sauvignon	5.0 ha.
Merlot	3.0 ha.

Caves Road, Willyabrup.
(Just over one kilometre south of the
junction with Metricup Road,
directly opposite Pierro.)

Postal address
PO Box 180
COWARAMUP 6284

Phone (097) 556 250
Fax   (097) 556 214

Hours of opening
11am to 4.30pm Tuesday to
Sunday

Flutes Cafe
11am to 4.30pm Tuesday to
Sunday, plus Saturday dinner.

Specialities
Preludes Art Gallery specialises in
wine artifacts (books, posters, art
work, glassware, decanters), has
the WA agency for the Hugh
Johnson Collection and the South
West agency for Riedel glassware.

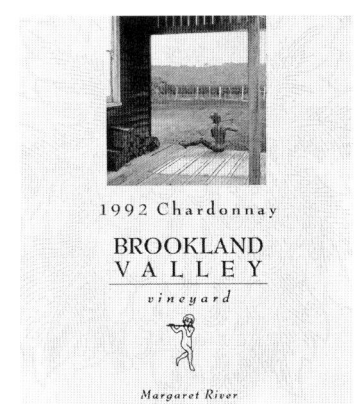

1992 Chardonnay

BROOKLAND
VALLEY
vineyard

Margaret River

Wines produced

Brookland Valley Chardonnay	*$17.50*
Brookland Valley Sauvignon Blanc	*$16.00*
Brookland Valley Cabernet Sauvignon, Merlot, Cabernet Franc *1991: 60% : 30% : 10%; 1992: 60% : 35% : 5%.*	*$17.00*
Flutes Red *Cabernet franc 90%, merlot 10%.*	*$15.00*

CAPE CLAIRAULT

FOR several years after moving to Margaret River to establish a vineyard in 1976, Ian Lewis spent a great deal of time working away from home as a geologist to make enough money to finance the project. In her first three years at Cape Clairault, Ani reared two small babies, had two more children and planted vines.

Two hectares of cabernet was planted in 1976 and riesling, semillon and sauvignon blanc were added the following year. The winery was completed in 1982, although the 1982 Cabernet Sauvignon was made before the roof was added.

In 1982, Ian fell from the roof of the winery, smashing his heel bone and was very ill for six months. When it came time to bottle the 1981 Cabernet, David Gregg, Erl Happ and John Brocksopp organised all the winemakers in the district to work two hours shifts to complete the task: a kindness that the Lewises remember with gratitude and affection.

When the winery won their first trophy for their superb 1982 Clairault Cabernet Sauvignon at the 1984 Canberra Show, the excitement was so great and money so scarce that Ani took the car to Perth with the four boys, collected Ian and they all drove to Canberra for the ceremony.

Ian made all the wines until 1988 when Jan and Mike Davies took over for two years. The vintages with the Davies gave Ian Lewis greater confidence in his own ability and knowledge of winemaking. Since then, Ian has made the wines with help from Peter Stark.

Additional plantings during 1994 and 1995 will add almost five hectares of vines and the Lewises will be hoping that the winery is producing 150 tonnes well before the turn of the century.

The best wines to come from Cape Clairault (pronounced to rhyme with 'halt') are The Clairault, the top red from the property each year, and the Sauvignon Blanc. The 1988 Cape Clairault Sauvignon Blanc won two trophies at the Sheraton Awards including Best Wine of the Show and the 1986 Clairault Cabernet won the trophy for Best Red Wine.

FORRESTAL FAVOURITE

1990 The Clairault
The best red produced by the winery. It has delicate, red cherry and spicy oak characters, rich, sweet redcurrant fruit and a soft finish that lingers. This is a fine, elegant, well-balanced red which has the weight, power and structure to reward cellaring.

Henry Road, Willyabrup.
(From Caves Road, take Abbey Farm
Road and turn right into Pusey
Road, then right into Henry Road.
Off Bussell Highway, take Wildwood
Road to Abbey Farm Road or
Harmans Mill Road to Pusey Road)

Postal address
CMB CARBUNUP RIVER 6280

Phone (097) 556 225
Fax   (097) 556 229

Hours of opening
10am to 5pm daily.

Specialities
Riedel glassware, books, Bordex
wineracks, Rapid Ice (to chill wines
for picnics), waiter's friend
corkscrew, a book by Ani Lewis 'I
want to plant a vineyard but I don't
know where to start' ($10) A hot
towel is provided in winter and a
cold towel in summer at the cellar
door. The toilet is not to be missed.

Owners
Ani and Ian Lewis

Winemaker
Ian Lewis

Established
1976

Production
90 tonnes
3,500 cases (1993)
6,000 cases (1994)

Area planted
9.30 ha.

Varieties planted

Chardonnay	0.25 ha.
Sauvignon Blanc	3.15 ha.
Semillon	1.50 ha.
Riesling	0.70 ha.
Cabernet Franc	0.50 ha.
Cabernet Sauvignon	2.30 ha.
Merlot	0.45 ha.
Touriga & Cinsault	0.20 ha.

Wines produced

Cape Clairault Sauvignon Blanc	*$17.00*
Cape Clairault Semillon Sauvignon Blanc	*$15.50*
Cape Clairault The Clairault 1991: cabernet sauvignon 51%, merlot 43%,cabernet franc 6%.	*$22.00*
Cape White A slightly sweet, sauvignon blanc/semillon blend.	*$13.00*
Cape Pink A slightly sweet blend of cabernet and merlot.	*$13.00*
Cape Red Cabernet sauvignon 80% merlot 15% cabernet franc 5%.	*$13.00*
Cape Late Harvest A sweet, luscious riesling.	*$13.00*
1990 Cape Clairault Vintage Port Made from cabernet sauvignon.	*$17.00*

CELLAR DOOR ONLY

Cape Clairault Claireau   (375ml) *$19.00*
A rich sweet fortified made from botrytised riesling and/or semillon.

CAPE MENTELLE

CAPE Mentelle was one of the first vineyards in the region when it was established by the Hohnen family in 1970. It took its name from the nearby cape which the eighteenth century French explorers had called after the Mentelle brothers: geographer Edmunde and cartographer François-Simon.

Cape Mentelle hit the national spotlight by winning Australia's most prestigious award, the Jimmy Watson Trophy, in consecutive years with the 1982 and 1983 Cape Mentelle Cabernets. This feat not only put the winery on the map but gave the Margaret River region its best ever marketing boost. At its peak, the 1982 showed rich, ripe berry fruit beautifully integrated with charry oak, great concentration and depth of flavour while the 1983 is still drinking beautifully thanks to its huge tannin structure which made it fairly unapproachable when young. It has great density, intense blackcurrant and spicy oak characters, a velvety texture and a firmish, dry finish.

David Hohnen, who made those legendary reds, is the driving force behind Cape Mentelle. He remains closely involved in the viticulture and winemaking although the talented John Durham has had the day to day responsibility for winemaking since 1984. Durham has steadily refined the Cape Mentelle reds and produced some impressive whites: the Semillon Sauvignon Blanc is the equal of any in the region and the Chardonnay is among the region's top half dozen wines of that variety.

The cabernets produced in the nineties are the best ever from the property while the shiraz, typically, is tightly structured with vibrant fruit and powerful oak handling that needs time to be seen at its best. The zinfandel is a massively concentrated wine of huge dimension which has a loyal band of supporters.

In 1985, David Hohnen set up Cloudy Bay as a sister company to Cape Mentelle in Malborough and helped put New Zealand sauvignon blanc on the world map. In 1988, Veuve Clicquot Ponsardin showed confidence in the region by becoming the majority shareholder in Cape Mentelle.

FORRESTAL FAVOURITE

1993 Chardonnay
Awarded the Chairman's Trophy for best wine of the Sheraton Awards, this delicious white is very clean and fresh with intense melon, peach, toasty oak and barrel ferment characters. The palate is soft, fine, fruity and powerful and the finish is dry and oaky. It's an outstanding youthful wine that will develop with even short term cellaring.

Owners
Veuve Clicquot Ponsadin (80%)
David Hohnen (20%)

Chief Executive
David Hohnen

Winemaker
John Durham

Viticulturist
Brenton Air

Established
1970

Production
870 tonnes
30,000 cases (1993)
45,000 cases (1994)

Area planted
40 ha.
Cape Mentelle also sources fruit from
56.2 hectares on the Chapman
Brook, Emerald Park, McHenry and
Ironstone Vineyards.

Varieties planted

	Grown on the Estate	Other Vineyards
Chardonnay		17.2 ha.
Chenin Blanc	0.6 ha.	3.3 ha.
Sauvignon Blanc	4.6 ha.	9.8 ha.
Semillon	7.6 ha.	7.5 ha.
Cabernet Sauv.	15.4 ha.	6.6 ha.
Grenache		1.5 ha.
Merlot	4.8 ha.	7.4 ha.
Shiraz	5.6 ha.	1.5 ha.
Zinfandel	1.4 ha.	1.4 ha.

MAP 5: E3   p155

Wallcliffe Road, Margaret River.
*(Turn right into Wallcliffe Road off
Bussell Highway at the top
(southern end) of the town of
Margaret River. The winery
entrance is just over 3km from the
township.
From Caves Road, the winery is
about 2km along Wallcliffe Road.)*

Postal address
 PO Box 110
 MARGARET RIVER 6285

 Phone (097) 573 266
 Fax   (097) 573 233

Hours of opening
 10am to 5pm daily

CAPE MENTELLE

CHARDONNAY 1994

Wines produced

Cape Mentelle Chardonnay	*$22.95*
Cape Mentelle Georgiana A blend of chenin blanc and semillon.	*$12.80*
Cape Mentelle Semillon Sauvignon Blanc	*$15.95*
Cape Mentelle Cabernet Sauvignon	*$28.50*
Cape Mentelle Cabernet Merlot From the Trinders Vineyard.	*$15.95*
Cape Mentelle Shiraz	*$17.50*
Cape Mentelle Zinfandel	*$17.50*

CHAPMAN'S CREEK

PERTH born and educated, Tony Lord began his career as a journalist in his home town firstly with the *West Australian* and then as news editor of radio station 6PM, before setting out in 1970 to forge a career on Fleet Street. In 1975, he bought the mailing list of a low circulation wine magazine from the receivers and, working on a shoe string budget, started *Decanter*. Twenty years later, many believe this to be the world's best wine magazine. During that time Tony Lord, as editor and then publisher, travelled extensively visiting vineyards in every major wine producing nation (except Russia and Cyprus).

While with *Decanter*, Lord reported on the Australian wine industry and developed an affection for the Margaret River which he claimed was 'the finest boutique wine region in Australia.' Following an offer from United Newspapers that was 'too good to refuse', Tony Lord sold his share in *Decanter* in 1991. However, he remained with the magazine for two years to honour a contract which gave the new owners continuity of management. As soon as his commitments to *Decanter* were finished, Lord returned to Perth to put into practice in his own vineyard what he had learnt about the wine industry over twenty years as a journalist.

His Chardonnay, Chenin Blanc and Cabernet Merlot will be produced from the vineyard but the Riesling, Shiraz and Port will be purchased from outside the region. The first riesling was made with fruit from Frankland River, there was no 1994, and the next vintage will come from either Mount Barker or another Margaret River vineyard. The shiraz is sourced from Capel just north of the boundary of the Margaret River region. The port is a blend of several vintages made from grapes grown in the Barossa Valley with some material up to 15 years old. Unusually for an Australian tawny port, it is made from the Portuguese variety, touriga: in fact, Tony Lord believes that it is the only 100% touriga port produced in Australia.

Lord says that the model for his chenin blanc is that of the South African winery, KWV, which produces a soft, floral and fruity wine with a high level of residual sugar. He is excited by his 1994 Cabernet Merlot which he describes as having attractive, blackcurrant flavours and soft tannins but with structure.

Owner
  Tony Lord
Chief Executive
  Tony Lord
Cellar Door Manager
  Chris Leach
Winemaker
  Maria Melsom at Driftwood
Established
  1992
Production
  60 tonnes
Area planted
  10.0 ha.
Varieties planted

Chardonnay	3.6 ha.
Chenin Blanc	2.0 ha.
Sauvignon Blanc	0.8 ha.
Semillon	0.8 ha.
Cabernet Sauvignon	2.0 ha.
Merlot	0.4 ha.

MAP 3: H4   **p153**

Yelverton Road, Willyabrup.
  (Turn off Bussell Highway into
  Yelverton Road.
  From Caves Road, turn down
  Metricup and left into Pusey Road
  and right into Yelverton Road.)

Postal address:
  8 College Road,
  CLAREMONT 6010

Phone: (097) 557 545
Fax: (097) 557 571

Hours of opening:
  Daily 10.30am - 5.00pm Dec to
  May: winter hours are likely to be
  11am - 4pm, daily.

Wines produced

Chapman's Creek Chardonnay	$16
Chapman's Creek Riesling	$10
Chapman's Creek Cabernet Sauvignon	$15
Chapman's Creek Cabernet Merlot	$20
Chapman's Creek Shiraz	$16
Chapman's Creek Port	$25

CULLEN

THE Cullen family were among the viticultural pioneers of the Margaret River when they planted cabernet sauvignon, malbec, riesling and traminer on their property in 1971. Subsequent plantings in 1976 of sauvignon blanc and merlot were the first for these varieties in the district.

In the early years, Dr Kevin Cullen was the driving force behind the winery but as he became absorbed in the long term research involved in the Busselton Health Survey, Di Cullen took over management. In 1981, she became winemaker, a role she carried out with distinction until handing responsibility to her daughter, Vanya, in 1989.

Vanya had been involved with the Cullen wines since 1984 and had worked closely with her mother before taking over. Her talent for winemaking shows sympathy for and understanding of the vineyard.

Cullen wines are among the region's best. The Cabernet Merlot and Chardonnay are outstanding. The Sauvignon Blanc is distinctive: it is picked ripe to give intensity and palate richness and aged in new French and German oak and has a unique, woody style that has a loyal following. The Pinot Noir has rich, complex, smokey, gamey characters and great power.

In the early days, a small amount of malbec (usually 10%) was blended with the cabernet but, with the 1982 vintage, Di Cullen decided to soften the wine with the addition of merlot. In most years since then, the blend has been cabernet sauvignon (60%), merlot (30%) and cabernet franc (10%) and is more approachable on release while still retaining the structure and depth of flavour to age gracefully. With the vines now more than twenty years old, the Cullen reds have more complexity than before, are more intense and have greater depth of flavour.

FORRESTAL FAVOURITE

1991 Cabernet Merlot Reserve

The four vintages of Cullen Cabernet Merlot Reserve mark the pinnacle of their winemaking achievement and rank among the very best red wines produced in the Margaret River. An outstanding vintage was responsible for the stunning 1991 Cullen Cabernet Merlot Reserve which has the greatest intensity, depth and concentration of flavour of any of these wines. It is surprisingly supple for such a powerful red and has rich, opulent blackberry and spicy oak characters, a velvety texture, excellent weight and the structure and fine tannins to age for more than a decade.

Owners
Cullen family partnership

Chief Executive
Di Cullen

Winemaker
Vanya Cullen

Viticulturist
Dick Marcus

Established
1971

Production
160 tonnes
10,000 cases (1993)
10,000 cases (1994)

Area planted
28.4 ha.

Varieties planted
Chardonnay	9.7 ha.
Sauvignon Blanc	3.2 ha.
Semillon	1.4 ha.
Riesling	2.4 ha.
Cabernet Sauvignon	7.7 ha.
Pinot Noir	1.2 ha.
Cabernet Franc	0.4 ha.
Merlot	2.4 ha.

Caves Road, Willyabrup.
(Next to Vasse Felix, about 500 metres north of the junction of Caves Road and Harmans South Road)

Postal address
PO Box 17
COWARAMUP 6284

Phone (097) 555 277
Fax   (097) 555 550

Hours of opening
10am to 4pm daily

Cafe
Open 10am to 4pm daily for light lunches, morning and afternoon teas.

C U L L E N

MARGARET RIVER

Cabernet Sauvignon
Merlot
1992

PRODUCED & BOTTLED BY CULLEN WINES
CAVES ROAD, COWARAMUP, W.A.
PRODUCT OF AUSTRALIA

Wines produced

Chardonnay	$25
Cullen Classic Dry White Sauvignon blanc, semillon, chardonnay, riesling blend.	$15
Cullen Sauvignon Blanc	$22
Cullen Semillon	$20
Cullen Blanc de Noir A sweet fruity table wine made from cabernet.	$14
Cullen Pinot Noir	$15
Cullen Cabernet Merlot	$25
Cullen Cabernet Merlot Reserve	$30
Cullen Botrytis Semillon Sauvignon Blanc	(750ml) $25
Cullen Late Harvest Cabernet A sweetish merlot and pinot.	$14

DEVIL'S LAIR

THE driving force behind Devil's Lair, Phil Sexton, has had a huge impact on the hospitality industry in Western Australia over the past decade by developing the boutique brewery, Matilda Bay, and many of Perth's best brasseries.

The first vines, planted in 1980, failed because of lack of water and because the gravel soil would not retain moisture. Plantings in 1983 struggled until a dam was built on a neighbour's property to supply supplementary water. By 1988, 14 hectares of vines were reasonably well established.

In that year, Phil Sexton bought 81 hectares adjoining the property and work began on a huge 350 megalitre dam. At Devil's Lair, supplementary water is vital during the first four years of the vines' life but the older sections of the vineyard no longer need to be irrigated.

Although the first commercial crop was produced from the vineyard in 1988, no wines appeared under the Devil's Lair label until the 1990 vintage.

Devil's Lair, named for a nearby cave in which the fossilised remains of a Tasmanian tiger were found, is currently undergoing a period of major expansion: four more hectares of chardonnay will come into production this year and a further 2.8 hectares of sauvignon blanc in 1997.

Devil's Lair is unquestionably among the very best of the newer wineries in the region. Their wines are in short supply and are mainly sold from the mailing list or through restaurants.

The 1990 Cabernet won Australia's most valuable show trophy as best wine at the 1992 SGIO Awards, a feat repeated two years later by the 1993 Pinot Noir.

FORRESTAL FAVOURITES

1990 Cabernet Sauvignon
Has spicy, cherry and mint characters, amazing suppleness and an almost velvety texture, richness and concentration of flavour and soft, fine grain tannins.

1992 Chardonnay
Has intense, passionfruit characters with hints of citrus, grapefruit and toasty oak and finishes with a crisp, dry acidity. This powerful wine has good depth, is complex and is among the best chardonnays from the region.

1993 Pinot Noir
The nose shows perfumed dark cherry, gamey, mushroomy, charry oak aromas, is soft, round and generous, rich and concentrated and has impressive weight, great depth of flavour and a long, lingering finish. This is a classy wine that adds a dimension to pinot from Margaret River: it is vibrant, complex and intense.

Rocky Road, Witchcliffe
(Take the Bussell Highway south
from Margaret River. Rocky Road is
13 km from the southern boundary
of the township and past
Witchcliffe. Travel just under 2 km
down Rocky Road, take the first
turn right after the bitumen ends,
and first right again.)

Postal address
42 Henry Street
FREMANTLE 6160

Phone (09) 336 3262
Mobile (018) 943 392
Fax   (09) 336 3263

No cellar door.
Visits by appointment only.
Cellar door on Bussell Highway,
due to be opened mid 1995.

Owners
 Philip and Allison Sexton

Chief Executives
 Philip and Allison Sexton

Winemaker
 Janice McDonald

Consultant
 Gary Baldwin

Viticulturist
 Simon Robertson

Established
 1981

Production
 280 tonnes
 10,000 cases (1993)
 13,000 cases (1994)

Area planted
 35.0 ha.

Varieties planted

Chardonnay	12.0 ha.
Sauvignon Blanc	3.0 ha.
Cabernet Franc	1.0 ha.
Cabernet Sauvignon	9.5 ha.
Merlot	2.0 ha.
Petit Verdot	1.0 ha.
Pinot Noir	6.5 ha.

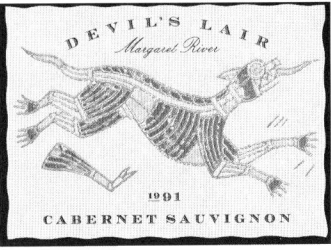

Wines produced *MAIL ORDER PRICES*

Devils Lair Chardonnay	*$20.00*
Devils Lair Sauvignon Blanc	*$17.50*
Devils Lair Cabernet Merlot	*$25.00*
Devils Lair Pinot Noir	*$25.00*

DRIFTWOOD ESTATE

WHAT started out as a weekend retreat for property developer, Tom Galopoulos, is in the process of becoming one of the most imposing winery, restaurant and cellar door complexes in the Margaret River. Galopoulos bought the land on which Driftwood Estate now stands in 1987, and remembering his Greek grandfather's love of his own wines, planted a few vines as a hobby. By 1989, he had decided to develop a commercial vineyard and, over the next four years, almost eighteen hectares were planted.

To get ideas for his 200 seat brasserie, Galopoulos toured California, France, Italy and Greece looking at winery restaurants. Viewed from Caves Road, it is not apparent that the restaurant has a superb outlook, through its glass wall, over the estate's vineyard to the south.

In establishing Driftwood, money has been no object and the winery's equipment is state-of-the-art. Winemaker, Maria Melsom, states that her mission is to concentrate on the vineyard in the expectation that growing quality fruit will make it easy to produce top class wines. It is expected that as further areas of the vineyard come into production and as yields improve with vine maturity, the present plantings will deliver a crop in the vicinity of 200 tonnes within five years or so.

The first vintages of Driftwood wines show the imprint of young vines but enough promise to suggest that the future is indeed bright. The Cabernet is soft and fruity, clean and fresh, of light to medium weight, straightforward but flavoursome: an easy drinking wine. The Chardonnay is quite oaky but is otherwise well made while the Semillon Chardonnay is clean and fresh with subtle flavours and reasonable weight. The Classic White will appeal to those who enjoy sweetish wines.

FORRESTAL FAVOURITE

1993 Semillon

Driftwood has had pleasing success with their first wine at the 1994 International Wine Challenge run by the London based magazine, Wine. *Their 1993 Semillon was awarded a commendation by the international panel. It is an impressive white showing good varietal definition and weight as well as richness and concentration of flavour.*

Because only limited quantities were produced, it will not be released commercially. It does, however, show the potential of the vineyard.

Owners
Tom and Helen Galopoulos

Chief Executive
Tom Galopoulos

Winemaker
Maria Melsom

Established
1989

Production
58 tonnes

Area planted
17.5 ha.

Varieties planted

Chardonnay	3.5 ha.
Semillon	3.0 ha.
Cabernet Sauvignon	4.5 ha.
Pinot Noir	1.0 ha.
Merlot	1.5 ha.
Chenin Blanc	2.0 ha.
Shiraz	1.0 ha.
Verdelho	1.0 ha.

Caves Road, Willyabrup.
(On the west side of Caves Road, between Abbey Farm and Johnson Roads.)

Postal address:
PO Box 645
SCARBOROUGH 6019

Winery
Phone   (097) 556 323
Fax   (097) 556 343

Head office
Phone   (09) 245 1688
Fax   (09) 245 1688

It is anticipated that the tasting complex at Driftwood will be open by about July 1995.

Wines produced

Driftwood Estate Chardonnay	*$18*
Driftwood Estate Classic White 1994: semillon 50%, chardonnay 30%, chenin blanc 20%.	*$12*
Driftwood Estate Semillon	*$15*
Driftwood Estate Semillon Chardonnay 1994: semillon 75%, chardonnay 25%.	*$15*
Driftwood Estate Cabernet Sauvignon	*$18*
Driftwood Estate Classic Red An early release cabernet.	*$14*

EVANS AND TATE

EVANS and Tate is one of Western Australia's most dynamic wine companies having increased production from 300 tonnes in 1992 to 740 tonnes in 1994 with plans for further massive expansion over the next few years. The demand for grapes will only partly be satisfied by its purchase of the 100 hectare Lionel Vineyard, a former potato farm at Jindong in the north-east of the region. This will be planted with chardonnay, sauvignon blanc and semillon over the next three years.

Senior winemaker, Brian Fletcher, has enhanced his reputation by supervising this expansion while improving wine quality.

While the winery and head office remain in the Swan Valley, Redbrook has been the source of Evans and Tate's best wines and an important contributor to its multi-regional blends. The vineyard was bought in late 1974, and planted between 1975 and 1979.

More than any other single wine, the Evans and Tate Classic has been responsible for the popularity of Classic Dry Whites in Western Australia. It was launched in 1987 with the production of 500 cases of a Margaret River blend and has become a very popular restaurant white. Because of its success, the wine can no longer be sourced from the one region.

During the 1980s, many fine cabernets and shiraz were produced from the Margaret River. These have improved considerably since 1990 due largely to the aging of the vines and the greater use of high quality oak.

The Margaret River Chardonnay is consistently one of the best of this variety produced in the region. Outstanding trophy winning wines were produced from the 1986, 1988 and 1990 vintages, although these appeared to have aged prematurely. Brian Fletcher, believes that the outstanding 1993 Chardonnay will have greater aging potential than previous wines. Similarly, the Evans and Tate Margaret River Semillon is among the best examples of this style produced in the area showing excellent varietal character, classy barrel ferment characters and the structure and natural acidity to age gracefully.

FORRESTAL FAVOURITE

1991 MR Cabernet Sauvignon
The best cabernet ever from this vineyard. It has a dark ruby colour and intense blackberry, dark cherry and charry oak characters, is supple and round with persistent, generous flavours a touch of extraction and firm tannins on its long, dry finish. This classy wine is complex, well-balanced and tightly structured.

Metricup Road, Willyabrup.
(Turn off Bussell Highway at
Metricup Road, 9km to vineyard
entrance.)
The Cellar door entrance is 500m
from the corner of Caves Road.

Owners
John, Toni and Franklin Tate

Chief Executive
Franklin Tate

Chief Winemaker
Brian Fletcher

Viticulturist
Murray Edmonds

Cellar Sales Supervisor
Cheryl Simpson

Established
1971

Production
740 tonnes
28,000 (1993)
43,000 cases (1994)

Area planted
19.27 ha. at Redbrook
4.00 ha. in the Swan Valley

Postal address
Swan Street
HENLEY BROOK 6055

Cellar door
Phone (097) 556 244

Head Office
Phone (09) 296 4666
Fax   (09) 296 1148

Hours of opening
10am to 5pm daily

Specialities
Tee shirts; bottle openers, bottle
covers; and a selection of older
vintages.

Varieties planted

Chardonnay	3.00 ha.	Cabernet Franc	0.40 ha.
Sauvignon Blanc	17.00 ha.	Cabernet Sauvignon	4.90 ha.
Semillon	4.80 ha.	Merlot	1.50 ha.
Verdelho	0.97 ha.	Shiraz	2.00 ha.

Wines produced   *CELLAR DOOR PRICES*

Evans and Tate Margaret River Chardonnay	*$31.00*
Evans and Tate Margaret River Semillon	*$17.50*
Evans and Tate Two Vineyards Chardonnay	*$15.50*
Evans and Tate Western Australian Classic Semillon 30%, sauvignon blanc 30%, verdelho 30%, chardonnay & chenin blanc 10%.	*$15.00*
Evans and Tate Margaret River Barrique 61 A merlot/cabernet blend.	*$18.50*
Evans and Tate Margaret River Cabernet Sauvignon	*$20.00*
Evans and Tate Margaret River Merlot	*$20.00*
Evans and Tate Margaret River Shiraz	*$18.50*
Evans and Tate Vintage Port	*$12.50*

FERMOY ESTATE

JOHN Anderson developed an interest in the wine industry and in the Margaret River region during his ten years as chairman of the Sandalford board. In 1984, he bought land opposite the Sandalford property with the intention of planting a vineyard and selling off the fruit. A change in plans, including a decision to build a winery, led to the involvement in the venture of a group of Perth businessmen.

One of Anderson's ancestors had played a significant part in founding the town of Fermoy in County Cork in the late eighteenth century. Legend has it that John Anderson made a spontaneous promise to call his winery after the town at a civic reception in his honour in Fermoy in 1985.

The Sheraton Awards have been a happy hunting ground for Fermoy as they won a gold medal with their first cabernet (the 1988), silvers with the subsequent two vintages and a gold with the 1991 Cabernet. Internationally, they have had success at the Intervin competition in Toronto winning silver medals with the 1991 Fermoy Estate Cabernet and their 1992 Merlot.

At this stage, the Cabernet and the Merlot are the most impressive of Fermoy Estate's wines with the latter being among the top three of the variety produced in Margaret River. The whites are clean, well-made wines that show good varietal definition. All the Fermoy wines represent good value for money.

FORRESTAL FAVOURITES

1992 Merlot
The 1991 performed superbly at the Perth Show and sold out overnight and the 1992 Fermoy Merlot is at least as good a wine. It is a rich, concentrated red which has an almost silky texture and yet plenty of power and substance. There are some restrained herbaceous characters and the wine is round and mouthfilling with substantial fine grain tannins.

1991 Cabernet Sauvignon
When winning the gold medal as best wine in its class at the 1994 Sheraton Awards, the judges praised it as being the most Bordeaux-like wine in the show. They were impressed with its varietal definition, sophisticated oak handling and complex cigar box, licorice, chocolate and stalky characters. While I admire the richness of spicy, berry fruit, the softness and roundness on the mid-palate, the velvety texture and the powerful concentration of flavour, I've felt that it has some extraction and bitterness on the finish which detracted from what is otherwise a complex, very reasonably priced wine.

Owners
John Anderson, Justin Seaward, Bill Caldow, Bill Mitchell, Antun Triglavcanin, Mike and Allison Kelly.

Chief Executive
John Anderson

Winemaker
Michael Kelly

Established
1985

Production
120 tonnes
5,500 cases (1993)
8,500 cases (1994)

Area planted
11 ha.

Varieties planted
Chardonnay	2 ha.
Sauvignon Blanc	2 ha.
Semillon	4 ha.
Cabernet Sauvignon	4 ha.
Merlot	2 ha.
Pinot Noir	2 ha.

Metricup Road, Willyabrup.
(Turn off Bussell Highway at Metricup Road, 8km to vineyard entrance.)

Postal address
PO Box 123
COWARAMUP 6284

Phone (097) 556 285
Fax   (097) 556 251

Hours of opening
10am to 4.30pm daily except Wednesdays.

Specialities
Tee shirts, rugby jumpers, corkscrews, foil cutters and tasting glasses.

Wines produced

Fermoy Estate Chardonnay	*$14.50*
Fermoy Estate Sauvignon Blanc	*$13.50*
Fermoy Estate Semillon *A wooded wine with 15% sauvignon blanc.*	*$13.50*
Fermoy Estate Cabernet Sauvignon	*$14.90*
Fermoy Estate Merlot	*$17.50*
Fermoy Estate Pinot Noir	*$17.50*

35

FOXHAVEN

AVID Hunt, who was originally from the Yallingup area, bought the Foxhaven block from his family in 1976 and planted vines in 1978. He had hoped to plant verdelho but had to opt for riesling instead. In 1981, Hunt added cabernet and, six years later, semillon. After the addition of another hectare in 1994, mainly of semillon but with a small amount of merlot, there will be no room for further expansion at Foxhaven.

Until 1990, David Hunt looked after the vineyard in his spare time while he worked in Perth as a director of a real estate valuation practice for Bailleu Knight Frank. He then ran a small valuation practice for two years while working on the vineyard part time and, since 1993, has been at Foxhaven full time.

The 1993 vintage was badly hit by an infestation of garden weevils and even though David Hunt sprayed and eliminated the pests, the crop of riesling and, to a lesser extent, the cabernet were significantly reduced.

The Foxhaven wines appear to be getting better with each vintage. The rieslings have been overpoweringly sweet and have lacked varietal definition until the most recent vintage.

The 1992 Foxhaven Cabernet Sauvignon is dominated by American oak, has some volatility and leathery characters but does have richness and softness on the mid-palate.

David Hunt is working hard to improve the vineyard and has great plans to expand the winery, buy new equipment, build an underground cellar and a new tasting room. If possible he would like to purchase another vineyard to help expand Foxhaven to a thousand case operation.

FORRESTAL FAVOURITE

1994 Riesling

Has a floral nose, some limey, citrusy flavours, is cleaner and much drier than previous vintages. It does have a touch of residual sugar on the finish but this is in better balance.

Canal Rocks Road, Yallingup.
(Turn into Canal Rocks Road from
Caves Road, cellar door entrance is
50 metres from the corner.)

Postal address
Canal Rocks Road
YALLINGUP 6282

Phone (097) 552 249
Fax   (09) 291 6052

Hours of opening
11am to 5pm weekends and school
holidays.

Owners
David and Libby Hunt

Winemaker
David Hunt

Established
1978

Production
9 tonnes
350 cases (1993)
500 cases (1994)

Area planted
3.40 ha.

Varieties planted

Riesling	1.50 ha.
Sauvignon Blanc	0.25 ha.
Semillon	0.90 ha.
Cabernet Sauvignon	0.50 ha.
Merlot	0.25 ha.

Wines produced

Foxhaven Estate Riesling	*$10*
Foxhaven Estate Semillon Sauvignon Blanc A blend of semillon 85%, sauvignon blanc 15%.	*$13*
Foxhaven Estate Cabernet Sauvignon	*$12*
Foxhaven Estate Cabernet Merlot	*$15*

GRALYN

GRAHAM and Merilyn Hutton were (and are) beef farmers who were impressed with the quality of the early wines from the region and decided to diversify during a flat time for the beef industry. They have not enlarged on their initial 4.5 hectare planting because, although their production is small, it is large enough to make Gralyn a commercial venture.

They handle all stages from viticulture and winemaking to sales. This involved a conscious choice in 1982 to concentrate on cellar door sales and maintain a personal involvement with their customers.

Today, almost all their sales are through the cellar door or through mail order custom which largely relies on initial contact made during a visit to Margaret River.

In 1978, Gralyn was the first in the area to operate a cellar door facility just ahead of Cullen. There was no established protocol at the time and so, for the first year, wine was sold without any tastings.

Today, the Australian wine industry depends for its success on being at the cutting edge of technology. This has not always been the case. In fact, the first qualified winemaker in the Margaret River region was Bob Cartwright who only became established at Leeuwin in 1978.

It is, therefore, hardly surprising that the lack of formal training did not deter or intimidate Graham and Merilyn Hutton. They did their first crush at Cullen and got feedback and advice from many locals including Bill Pannell at Moss Wood and Tony Devitt from the Agriculture Department. They read a great deal, attended seminars and learnt more with each passing vintage.

In 1979, Gralyn sold their first vintage port and since then fortified wines have become a significant part of their business. The Huttons believed that the red wines of Margaret River had all the attributes of good port and saw a niche in the market that few others were exploiting.

Many of the table wines and the White, Pink and Ruby Ports will appeal to those who enjoy sweet wines.

FORRESTAL FAVOURITE

Gralyn Vintage & Tawny Ports

I am particularly impressed by the Gralyn vintage and tawny ports which are well made, have great richness, concentration of flavour, complexity and consequently are deservedly popular.

Owners / Winemakers
  Graham and Merilyn Hutton

Established
  1975

Production
  30 tonnes
  1500 cases (1993)
  1500 cases (1994)

Area planted
  4.5 ha.

Varieties planted

Cabernet Sauvignon	2.4 ha.
Shiraz	0.6 ha.
Semillon	0.1 ha.
Riesling	1.4 ha.

Caves Road, Willyabrup.
  (Situated just over two km from either Metricup Road or Harmans South Road between Ribbon Vale and Cullen.)

Postal address
  Post Office
  COWARAMUP 6284

  Phone (097) 556 245
  Fax   (097) 556 245

Hours of opening
  10.30am to 4.30pm daily

Wines produced

Gralyn Riesling Semillon	$10
Gralyn Riesling	$10
Gralyn Spatlese Riesling	$10
Gralyn Spatlese Cabernet A sweet, unoaked cabernet.	$10
Gralyn Cabernet Nouveau An unoaked cabernet with a sweetish finish.	$10
Gralyn Shiraz	$10
Gralyn White Port Made from riesling.	$10
Gralyn Pink Port Made from cabernet sauvignon.	$10
Gralyn Ruby Port Made from cabernet sauvignon.	$10

SPECIAL RELEASES

Gralyn Auslese Riesling	(375ml) $15
Gralyn Liqueur White Port Made from riesling and aged in oak for a year.	$30
Michael Hutton Cabernet Vintage Port	$15
Bradley Hutton Vintage Port Made from cabernet and shiraz.	$15
1981 Gralyn Cabernet Vintage Port	$25
Gralyn Cabernet Tawny Port	(375ml) $25
Gralyn Hermitage Tawny Port Ten year old made from shiraz.	$25

GREEN VALLEY

ED and Eleonore Green are among a small band of dedicated wine lovers who have developed a Margaret River vineyard on busy weekends while leading another life in the city during the week. Eleonore is a dentist with the Public Health Department and Ed retired in January 1995 after 44 years as a weatherman, ultimately as the Bureau of Meteorology's manager of weather services for military and civil aviation.

The impetus to start a vineyard came from two unrelated circumstances. Ed and Eleonore missed their young girls so much on an expensive trip to Singapore and Malaysia in 1979 that they decided to make future holidays family affairs. They decided that it would be better to spend money on a permanent holiday home and so discussed a range of possibilities. At much the same time, Ed Green was forced by eyesight problems to withdraw from a part time MBA at Curtin University and felt in need of challenge to occupy his spare time.

After family discussions and consultation with the Agriculture Department, the Greens decided to look for land which would be suitable for a vineyard. A six month search led them further south than any established Margaret River vineyard to a former soldier settler farm at Forest Grove.

The vineyard has been planted one hectare every second year from 1980 until it reached its present size. The first crop came off the vines in 1986 and the first commercial harvest came in the following year as Muller Thurgau and Riesling was made at Vasse Felix.

Green Valley is a very cool site, gets plenty of cloud cover, and is not susceptible to frost or hail damage. It is, however, very dry and needs irrigation. In addition, it is adjacent to the Boranup Forest and so bird damage has been a significant problem.

Following his retirement from the Bureau of Meteorology, Ed Green plans to spend more time at Forest Grove. Among other things, he will improve canopy control and complete netting of the whole vineyard. This should enable him to delay picking grapes until they are fully ripe: a luxury that the birds have not allowed thus far.

FORRESTAL FAVOURITE

1992 Chardonnay
The 1992 Chardonnay is a clean, well-made white with melon, citrus and toasty oak characters, a hint of greenness, pleasant mid-palate softness and crisp acidity on the finish.

Sebbes Road, Forest Grove.
(Follow Bussell Highway 16 km
south of Margaret River through
Witchcliffe to Sebbes Road and turn
right. Green Valley is about 300
metres along Sebbes Road on the
left.)

Postal address
  2 Cornwall Street
  SWANBOURNE 6010

  Phone (09) 384 3131

Hours of opening
  10am to 6pm, Saturdays
  10 to 4pm, Sundays and public
  holidays

Owners
  Ed and Eleonore Green

Chief Executive
  Ed Green

Winemakers
  Jürg Muggli at Xanadu makes Muller
  Thurgau, Chardonnay and Dolce
  (from hand-picked grapes).
  Clive Otto at Vasse Felix makes
  Cabernet and Riesling (from
  machine picked grapes)

Established
  1980

Production
  25 tonnes
  1500 cases (1993)
  1800 cases (1994)

Area planted
  5.8 ha.

Varieties planted

Chardonnay	1.2 ha.
Chenin Blanc	0.2 ha.
Colombard	0.2 ha.
Muller Thurgau	0.4 ha.
Rhine Riesling	1.0 ha.
Cabernet Sauvignon	2.4 ha.
Merlot	0.4 ha.

Wines produced

Green Valley Chardonnay	*$15.50*
Green Valley Rhine Riesling	*$12.95*
Green Valley Muller Thurgau	*$10.50*
Green Valley Dolce	*$11.50*
A semi-sweet chenin blanc made from estate grown and purchased grapes.	
Green Valley Cabernet Sauvignon	*$17.50*

HAPPS

INSPIRED by John Gladstones's viticultural research which suggested that Margaret River would be an excellent area for growing grapes, school teacher and part time potter, Erl Happ, spent more than two years hunting for the site of a vineyard. In 1978, he found a 22 hectare property on a ridge overlooking Geographe Bay and persuaded the owner to sell.

During three months long service leave, Erl made mud bricks for a pottery and family home, supervised the building of both, and began planting the vineyard. After resigning from teaching in 1979, he worked in the pottery and winery until 1990 when increased production in the winery demanded his full attention.

Erl Happ is an innovator who thinks laterally and is always keen to experiment. This can be seen in the unique wine styles he has developed and in his recent purchase of a property at Karridale, to the south of Margaret River. There he has planted eleven hectares with seven varieties of white and fifteen of red grapes including many of which are rarely if ever seen in the region. These include the white varieties; furmint, viognier and marsanne, and the red varieties; graciano, gamay, tempranillo, nebbiolo, sangiovese and carignan.

The winery is well known for its merlots which are among the region's best: they are soft, rich and generous and ready to drink on release. For those interested in fortified reds, the Happs Fortis is a top quality wine made using Portuguese grape varieties while the Garnet, a fortified sweet red, has lovely, muscaty, raisiny characters, is soft and gently lush. The Fushia is Happs most popular wine: pale pink, delicately floral, clean and fresh with a gentle, sweet finish.

FORRESTAL FAVOURITES

1990 Merlot
Has lifted herbaceous, plummy and dark chocolate characters on the nose, is soft, round and generous, has good balance and reasonably firm tannins. It is a good food wine which will improve with short term cellaring.

1990 Shiraz
Having more bottle age than most current release shiraz has given the 1990 Happs Shiraz time to fill out and develop into a soft, round and generous red with an intense peppery nose and some spicy, green leaf and licorice characters. It has finesse as well as great concentration and richness of flavour.

Commonage Road, Dunsborough.
*(Just east of Dunsborough, turn off
Caves Road into Commonage Road
follow it for 6 km.)*

Postal address
Post Office
DUNSBOROUGH 6281

Phone *(097) 553 300*
Fax   *(097) 553 846*

Hours of opening
10am to 5pm daily

Specialities
Wine books and, tee shirts. Pottery
Studio run by Rika Rouw and Kim
Potter featuring a vast range
including: candlestick holders,
casserole dishes, coffee mugs, egg
cups, jars, lamps bases, vases,
zodiac symbols.

Owners
Erland and Roslyn Happ

Chief Executive
Erl Happ

Winemakers
Erl Happ, Frank Kittler

Established
1978

Production
150 tonnes
10,000 cases (1993)
11,000cases (1994)

Area planted
6.5 ha.

Varieties planted

Chardonnay	1.2 ha.		
Verdelho	1.3 ha.		
Cabernet Sauvignon	1.2 ha.	Brown Muscat	0.2 ha.
Merlot	1.2 ha.	Touriga, Tinta Cao	
Shiraz	1.2 ha.	& Sousão	0.2 ha.

Wines produced

Happs Chardonnay	*$16*
Happs Semillon Verdelho A slightly sweet blend.	*$13*
Happs Verdelho A sweet white.	*$13*
Happs Fuchsia A slightly sweet pink made from cabernet, merlot & shiraz.	*$11*
Happs Topaz	*$11*
Happs Shiraz	*$11*
Happs Merlot	*$16*
Happs Cabernet Merlot	*$15*
Happs Fortis A fortified vintage port style aged in wood for 2 years.	*$15*
Happs 10 Year Fortis	*$25*
Happs Garnet A fortified red dessert wine made from muscat.	*(375ml) $9*
Happs Pale Gold A sweet white port.	*$12*
Happs Old Bronze A light-bodied muscat aged in oak for 2 years.	*(375ml) $11*

HAY SHED HILL

I N Hay Shed Hill, the Willyabrup Valley has an attractive new state-of-the-art winery quite unlike any other in the region and one of the most impressive cellar door outlets I've seen anywhere

Originally established in 1973 as Sussex Vale by the Middletons, the vineyard was in need of a great deal of work when purchased by Liz and Barry Morrison in June 1989. They were attracted to the property by its Willyabrup location, its established vines and the cute white house and hayshed on the property. A viticultural analysis showed its promise but the soil needed rehabilitation and the vines retrellising before its full potential could be harnessed.

Since taking over, the Morrisons have planted pinot noir and added to the plantings of sauvignon blanc, semillon and chardonnay.

Atypically, Liz and Barry decided to wait until they were satisfied with the quality of the fruit coming from the property before making white wines of their own. They sold off fruit for three vintages and were rewarded when winemaker, John Smith, produced some fresh, clean, flavoursome whites with distinct varietal character in 1993.

When those wines were ready, the winery was opened, more than four years after the property had been bought.

A wicked sense of humour lies behind the commissioning of a corrugated iron flag, sculptured by Adelaide artist, Bruce Howard, which flies over the winery. This was inspired by Leunig's cartoon which recommended that the new national flag be made of corrugated iron because almost everyone in the country had fought under it.

A Cabernet Sauvignon has been made each year since the property was purchased. Each shows the benefit of being made from twenty year old vines:, having a velvety texture, richness, concentration and depth of flavour.

Of the wines released so far, the Semillon and the Sauvignon Blanc are the most impressive and approach the quality of the best in the region. Pitchfork Pink is a unique and popular blend being fresh, fruity and just a touch sweet.

FORRESTAL FAVOURITE

1993 Semillon

Fifty per cent of the blend for the 1993 Hay Shed Hill Semillon was matured in new French oak and consequently the wine has some toasty, nutty, barrel-ferment flavours to complement its regional grassiness. It is fresh and lively now but will reward cellaring by developing some rich, mature honeyed characters.

Harmans Mill Road, Willyabrup.
(Off Bussell Highway, take Harmans
Mill Road for just over 4 km.
Off Caves Road, take Harmans
Road South for about 6 km.)

Postal address
   CMB
   COWARAMUP 6284

Winery
   Phone (097) 556 234
   Fax   (097) 556 305

Head Office
   Phone (09) 383 1064
   Fax   (09) 383 1064

Hours of opening
   10.30am to 5pm on weekends,
   public and school holidays.

Specialities
   Tee shirts, rugby jumpers, caps,
   cards and pepper grinders.

Owners
   Liz and Barry Morrison

Chief Executive
   Liz Morrison

Winemaker
   Peter Stanlake

Consultant
   Mike and Jan Davies

Vineyard Manager
   Will Russell

Established
   1974

Production
   40 tonnes
   1900 cases (1993)
   3000 cases (1994)

Area planted
   13 ha.

Varieties planted

Chardonnay	4.0 ha.
Muscat of Alexandra	0.5 ha.
Semillon	1.5 ha.
Sauvignon Blanc	2.0 ha.
Cabernet Sauvignon	5.0 ha.
Pinot Noir	1.5 ha.

Wines produced

Hay Shed Hill Semillon	*$14*
Hay Shed Hill Sauvignon Blanc	*$13*
Hay Shed Hill Pitchfork Pink	*$11*
A slightly sweet rosé style made from cabernet 90% & muscat of Alexandria 10%.	
Hay Shed Hill Cabernet Sauvignon	*$15*
Hay Shed Hill Group 20 Cabernet *A light bodied,unwooded style.*	*$12*

45

LEEUWIN ESTATE

THE Horgan family bought their property in 1969 as a Poll Hereford ranch but after meeting the influential Californian winemaker, Robert Mondavi, in 1973, they entered a joint venture arrangement to develop a winery. During the four years that this arrangement lasted, Mondavi advised them on setting up the winery and vineyard.

The sole objective of Denis and Trisha Horgan in setting up Leeuwin Estate was to produce wines that would rank with the world's best. They should be well pleased with their achievement..

Much of the success of the Leeuwin wines is due to the quality of vineyard management and the close working relationship between viticulturist, John Brocksopp, and winemaker, Bob Cartwright, both of whom have been at Leeuwin since its beginning.

The Leeuwin Winery Complex is one of the show pieces of Margaret River and the annual open air concert, is one of the highlights of the state's social calendar.

The 1981 Art Series Chardonnay first put Margaret River on the international map when it topped a tasting of chardonnays from around the world run by the British wine magazine, *Decanter*. The 1986 repeated this feat. Another British magazine, *Wine*, rated the Leeuwin Chardonnay among the world's top one hundred wines and the Italian Slow Food Movement's *Guide to the Wines of the World* includes it among Australia's top eight and in the world's top 150 wines. By any standards, it is a great white and well worth its asking price.

Each year since the first vintage in 1980, the winery has produced Australia's best or one of its best chardonnays. These have been consistent, outstanding and age remarkably well. The most impressive have been the 1982, 1987, 1986 and the 1990. Both the 1991 and 1992 are outstanding.

The Art Series Pinot Noirs and the Sauvignon Blancs are well-made, flavoursome wines with distinct varietal character. The Prelude Chardonnay represents good value for money.

The Art Series Cabernet Sauvignon is improving with each vintage and, from 1989 onwards, ranks among the region's best. The 1991 is the best red from the winery and is, I believe, one of the greatest cabernets ever from Margaret River.

FORRESTAL FAVOURITE

1990 Art Series Chardonnay
Has great intensity and power yet is elegant, harmonious and complex with nutty, peachy, melony characters and an almost chewy texture.

Stevens Road, Margaret River.
(Turn off Bussell Highway 4km
south of Margaret River onto
Gnaraway Road, and after just
over 3 km, turn left into Stevens
Road and follow it for almost 4 km.
From Caves Road, drive 3 km down
Boodjidup Road, turn into Gnara-
wary Road and almost immediately
into Stevens Road.)

Postal address
  PO Box 724
  FREMANTLE 6010

Winery
  Phone (097) 576 253
  Fax   (097) 576 364

Head Office
  Phone (09) 430 4099
  Fax   (09) 430 5687

Hours of opening
  10am to 4.30pm daily
  Tours of the winery with tutored
  tasting at 11am, 1pm, 3pm. $6.

Restaurant
  12 to 2.30pm daily and from 7pm
  Saturday evening.

Specialities
  Sweat shirts, tee shirts, local wood-
  work and jewellery, chutneys, jams
  & mustards from Newtown House,
  display of Art Series paintings.

Owners
  Rural Developments P/L

Chief Executive
  Denis Horgan

Winemaker
  Bob Cartwright

Production Manager
  John Brocksopp

Established
  1974

Production
  500 tonnes
  35,000 cases (1993)
  35,000 cases (1994)

Area planted
  92.61 ha.

Varieties planted

Chardonnay	20.21 ha.
Riesling	27.87 ha.
Sauvignon Blanc	4.26 ha.
Semillon	0.10 ha.
Cabernet Sauvignon	27.77 ha.
Malbec	2.60 ha.
Merlot	1.00 ha.
Petit Verdot	1.50 ha.
Pinot Noir	7.30 ha.

Wines produced

Leeuwin Estate Art Series Chardonnay	*$38.50*
Leeuwin Estate Prelude Chardonnay	*$19.00*
Leeuwin Estate Prelude Blended White Chardonnay, sauvignon blanc, riesling.	*$12.50*
Leeuwin Estate Art Series Riesling	*$14.50*
Leeuwin Estate Art Series Sauvignon Blanc	*$26.00*
Leeuwin Estate Art Series Cabernet Sauvignon	*$29.95*
Leeuwin Estate Prelude Cabernet Sauvignon	*$18.50*
Leeuwin Estate Art Series Pinot Noir	*$29.95*
Leeuwin Estate Late Harvest Riesling	*$11.50*

LENTON BRAE

WHEN Jack Gutherie had the original Moss Wood property sub divided in 1982, two blocks remained as Moss Wood. A Perth-based architect, Bruce Tomlinson, bought the southern block adjacent to Caves Road while the northern block became Moss Brothers.

The distinctive name of the winery has connections with the Tomlinson family. When Bruce's great grandparents settled in Perth in 1884, they named their house 'Lenton' after the district in Nottingham from which they came. In Scotland a 'brae' is a little hill and as this infers well-drained land, Bruce decided that it was a suitable descriptor for the vineyard.

Bruce Tomlinson first planted the property in 1982 and worked on it on weekends and in holidays for the next eight years. By 1990, the vineyard was producing 30 tonnes of fruit and needed more time spent on things like canopy management and trellising.

The first two vintages were made at Redgate and, although roofless, the winery was able to function during the 1989 vintage when the wines were made by Rob Bowen. The winery was fully ready by the next year and, with Bowen in New Zealand, Tomlinson managed vintage with the help of Roseworthy graduate, Sarah Watts.

Bruce Tomlinson says that after this vintage it became obvious that he needed to be at Lenton Brae full time. He also decided to involve more experienced people in the operation of the winery.

As the Tomlinson children had grown up and left home, Bruce retired from architecture and he and Jeanette moved to Lenton Brae.

Two wines have had outstanding success. The first red, the 1988 Cabernet Sauvignon, won the trophy for the best wine in the 1990 SGIO Exhibition while the 1992 Chardonnay won three trophies including best WA wine at the 1993 Perth Show.

Unusually, the cellar door is set amid the hustle and bustle of the winery with the laboratory along its back wall and opposite some superb stainglass windows.

FORRESTAL FAVOURITES

1993 Chardonnay
A gentle soft wine with delicate citrus characters, some mid-palate intensity and a fresh, clean and crisp finish.

1992 Cabernet Sauvignon
This is a big, powerful red which has a perfumed spicy nose, some herbaceous characters on the mid-palate and quite firm, fine grained tannins.

Caves Road, Willyabrup.
*(Just north of the junction with
Metricup Road.)*

Postal address
PO Box 500
MARGARET RIVER 6285

Phone (097) 556 255
Fax   (097) 556 268

Hours of opening
10am to 6pm daily

Specialities
Tee shirts, sweat shirts and
Margaret River cheeses.

Owners
A private company involving Bruce
and Jeanette Tomlinson and others.

Chief Executive
Bruce Tomlinson

Winemaker
Edward Tomlinson

Consultant
Gary Baldwin of Oenotec

Viticulturist:
Bruce Tomlinson

Consultant:
Di Davidson

Established
1982

Production
95 tonnes
5000 cases (1993)
5500 cases (1994)

Area planted
10.2 ha.

Varieties planted

Chardonnay	2.5 ha.
Sauvignon Blanc	2.0 ha.
Semillon	1.2 ha.
Cabernet Franc	0.3 ha.
Cabernet Sauvignon	3.2 ha.
Merlot	0.8 ha.
Petit Verdot	0.2 ha.

MARGARET RIVER

Wines produced

Lenton Brae Chardonnay	*$16.00*
Lenton Brae Sauvignon Blanc	*$12.50*
Lenton Brae Semillon-Sauvignon Blanc	*$12.50*
Lenton Brae Cabernet Merlot	*$12.50*
Lenton Brae Cabernet Sauvignon	*$16.50*
Lenton Brae Late Harvest *A sweet blend of semillon/sauvignon blanc.*	*$10.50*

MOSS BROTHERS

J EFF Moss always wanted to be a winemaker but came to owning a winery in Margaret River by an indirect route. He worked for Mildara and Hardys in the Riverland, grew grapes on his own property there for 16 years. and then worked for Houghton in the Swan Valley.

While working there, Jeff Moss wondered what to do with his weekends. He eventually focussed on Margaret River and looked for a small affordable block.

When Bill Pannell negotiated the purchase of the Moss Wood land in 1969, the owner, Jack Gutherie, had given him first option over the entire block. In 1982, Pannell released Gutherie from that option and the northern block adjoining Caves Road was sold to Jeff Moss.

From the autumn of 1985, the Moss family spent their weekends and holidays clearing the block. Jeff and his sons, David and Peter slept in the barrel room at Moss Wood each weekend until they moved to Margaret River in 1987.

David Moss worked at Moss Wood in 1987 and 1988 and Peter Moss made stainless steel tanks to fund the development of the vineyard. Their sister, Jane, graduated from Roseworthy in 1991 a major achievement, as her husband was living in Melbourne at the time and her son, Alec, at 18 months, had become the youngest person to attend the College.

The name Moss Brothers has been the cause of some controversy because the winery has often been confused with nearby Moss Wood. Ironically, the name also marginalises their winemaker, Jane Moss, who comes from Melbourne for each vintage.

The best of the Moss Brothers wines is their Pinot Noir, with the 1991 vintage producing an outstanding example of the variety. The Moses Rock Red is a fresh, easy drinking wine that represents good value while the Bona Vista White has a silky texture and a sweetness that will appeal to many.

The approach to pricing wines at Moss Brothers is refreshing with lesser vintages being released at cheaper prices.

FORRESTAL FAVOURITES

1992 and 1993 Pinot Noir

Although the 1992 lacks the intensity of the previous vintage, it has distinct varietal character, some perfumed raspberry, strawberry aromas, is soft with medium weight and attractive cherry, berry flavours. The 1993 is lightly perfumed with attractive strawberry, red cherry and spice characters, and rich, soft, yet persistent, sweet fruit flavours.

Owners
The Moss Family (Fay and Jeff, Peter, David and Jane)

Chief Executives
Jeff and Fay Moss

Winemakers
Jane and David Moss

Viticulturist
David Moss

Established
1985

Production
80 tonnes
4000 cases (1993)
5500 cases (1994)

Area planted
6.5 ha.

Varieties planted

Chardonnay	1.0 ha.
Sauvignon Blanc	1.0 ha.
Semillon	1.4 ha.
Cabernet Franc	1.0 ha.
Merlot	1.0 ha.
Pinot Noir	1.4 ha.
Grenache	0.4 ha.

Caves Road, Willyabrup.
(Just north of the corner with Metricup Road, next to Lenton Brae.)

Postal address
PO Box 469
MARGARET RIVER 6285

Phone (097) 556 270
Fax   (097) 556 298

Hours of opening
10am to 6pm daily

Wines produced

Moss Brothers Chardonnay	*$19.50*
Moss Brothers Semillon Sauvignon Blanc	*$15.00*
Moss Brothers Moses Rock Red	*$12.00*
Cabernet franc 50%, pinot noir 20%, cabernet sauvignon 15%, merlot 10%, grenache 5%.	
Moss Brothers Pinot Noir	*$17.00*
Moss Brothers Cabernet Merlot	*$19.50*
CELLAR DOOR ONLY	
Bona Vista White	*$16.50*
Bona Vista Ruby	*$16.50*

MOSS WOOD

AFTER a decade of owner-ship by Keith and Clare Mugford, Moss Wood's reputation as one of the Australia's best boutique wineries is assured. Established by Bill and Sandra Pannell in 1969, this was the region's second winery. The first vintage of cabernet was in 1973, pinot noir and semillon in 1977 and chardonnay in 1980.

In 1978, Bill Pannell employed Roseworthy graduate, Keith Mugford and they worked closely together for several years until, in 1985, the Pannells decided to move on and so they sold Moss Wood to the Mugfords.

The Cabernet is the equal of any produced in the region and one of Australia's best. The influence of both the Pannell and Mugford eras is clear in the present day wines which show the additional benefit of mature vines. The benchmarks for the cabernets remain the wines made by Bill Pannell from 1975 to 1977. Recent experimentation with trellis management and soil conservation as well as prolonged skin contact and the addition of cabernet franc, merlot and petit verdot to the blend have produced wines of greater finesse and complexity.

The wines produced from their best vintages, the 1980, 1975, 1991, 1983, 1990 and 1985, have been among the greatest of the Margaret River reds.

The chardonnay, semillon and pinot are consistently among the region's most impressive. The early chardonnays showed distinct regional and varietal character and the ability to age well. However, since 1990 these have been more complex and more consistent. The semillons are less herbaceous than most others from Margaret River and they age particularly well.

In its time, the 1981 Moss Wood Pinot Noir was regarded as one of the best pinots ever produced in this country, although only the best bottles still look outstanding. The 1985, 1986 and 1991 vintages produced excellent wines which have distinct varietal character, richness and concentration of flavour, velvety texture and the ability to age gracefully.

FORRESTAL FAVOURITE

1992 Cabernet Sauvignon

This wine has lifted, redcurrant and spicy oak characters, long, rich, mulberry flavours, some earthiness and well-integrated, soft tannins. It has lively mouthfeel, fresh acidity and some smokey oak on the finish. Although it can be enjoyed while young for its fresh fruitiness, it will show greater complexity and depth of flavour after ten years cellaring.

Metricup Road, Willyabrup.
(On Metricup Road near the
junction with Caves Road. Just over
9km from Bussell Highway.)

Postal Address
PO Box 52
BUSSELTON 6280

Phone　(097) 556 266
Fax　　(097) 556 303

Tours and tastings by
appointment only.

Owners
　Keith and Clare Mugford

Winemaker
　Keith Mugford

Vineyard Manager
　Ian Bell

Production
　75 tonnes
　4,5000 cases (1993)
　4,500 cases (1994)

Area planted
　8.34 ha.

Varieties planted

Chardonnay	1.29 ha.
Semillon	1.35 ha.
Cabernet Franc	0.26 ha.
Cabernet Sauvignon	3.70 ha.
Merlot	0.03 ha.
Petit Verdot	0.26 ha.
Pinot Noir	1.45 ha.

Wines produced *MAIL ORDER PRICES*

Moss Wood Chardonnay	*$23.00*
Moss Wood Semillon	*$17.00*
Moss Wood Cabernet Sauvignon	*$24.00*
Moss Wood Cabernet Sauvignon (Special Reserve)	*$40.00*
Moss Wood Pinot Noir	*$22.50*

Magnums of the Cabernet Sauvignon are available to mail order customers.
Limit one per customer, $65 each.

PALMERS

DURING the late sixties, Steve Palmer worked for the R & I Bank as a farm adviser. He watched the fledgling wine industry with interest and, with a partner, bought a large Willyabrup property in 1972. After a proposed joint venture with Seppelt fell through, the partners subdivided the land and, in 1974, Evans and Tate bought the Redbrook Vineyard and Sandalford increased their block by a third. There was a further subdivision in 1980 and Pierro and Palmers were the result.

In the meantime, Steve Palmer had planted about two hectares of cabernet. The young vines were devastated by Cyclone Alby in 1977 only to reshoot and be decimated by a grasshopper plague. The vineyard was abandoned for a time while the Palmers built up the Remlap Stud at Myalup to pursue another of their loves, horse racing.

The successes of the Margaret River vignerons, lured the Palmers back into the wine industry and, during the eighties, Mike Peterkin at Pierro supervised the planting of the vineyard and managed it. The first commercial vintage took place in 1989. Initially, the whites were made by Mike Peterkin and the reds by Mike Davies but from 1994 all the wines are made by Eddie Price at Amberley.

The Palmers became involved in the Western Australian purchase of Sandalford in 1992, partly motivated by the desire to buy back the farm they had sold in 1974, but they withdrew after a short time to concentrate on their other interests.

The Palmer Chardonnays are very impressive. The 1992 won a gold medal and trophy as the best chardonnay at the 1993 Mt Barker Show and the 1993 won a gold medal in the following year. They are mainly sold in restaurants or to corporate clients and so are not as well known as they deserve to be. The best of the other wines is the Sauvignon Blanc, while the Cabernet is a pleasant, well-made, easy drinking red.

FORRESTAL FAVOURITES

1994 Chardonnay
A beautifully made wine with restrained melon and spicy oak aromas, rich, white peach and cashew flavours and gentle acidity on the finish. It is soft and round, has excellent weight and shows good balance between its classy oak and ripe fruit.

1994 Sauvignon Blanc
Clean, fresh and full flavoured with lively ripe, tropical fruit, guava and passionfruit characters. It is a soft, gentle wine with attractive sweet fruit and a crisp, dry finish that lingers.

Owners
Helen and Steve Palmer

Chief Executive
Helen Palmer

Winemaker
Eddie Price at Amberley Estate

Viticulturist
Kevin Richardson

Established
1977

Production
65 tonnes
3,000 cases (1993)
4,200 cases (1994)

Area planted
10.2 ha.

Varieties planted

Chardonnay	2.8 ha.
Sauvignon Blanc	2.0 ha.
Semillon	2.4 ha.
Cabernet Sauvignon	1.6 ha.
Merlot	1.2 ha.
Cabernet Franc	0.2 ha.

Caves Road, Willyabrup.
(Immediately south of the junction
with Metricup Road, next to Pierro)

Postal address
33 Cathedral Avenue
AUSTRALIND 6230

Phone   (097) 971 881
Mobile   (018) 916 952
Fax   (097) 972 534

There is no cellar door. Visits
may be possible by appointment.
For case lot orders, phone
(018) 916 952.

Wines produced

Palmers Chardonnay	$18.75
Palmers Classic A blend of chardonnay, sauvignon blanc and semillon.	$16.75
Palmers Sauvignon Blanc	$15.50
Palmers Semillon	$16.95
Palmers Cabernet Sauvignon	$19.95

PIERRO

IERRO'S Mike Peterkin is unique in the Margaret River in that he is the only doctor (among many involved in the industry) who is also a fully qualified winemaker and viticulturist.

While at Roseworthy, Peterkin came under the influence of Richard Smart whose ideas were then considered unfashionable but have since become accepted practice. Therefore his vineyard was closely planted on poor soil with irrigation playing an important part; the canopy is carefully managed to allow plenty of sunlight onto the leaves and the fruit to ensure optimum ripeness and to reduce herbaceousness. The poor, granite soil on the property serves to control the vigour of the vines with irrigation being available, not to increase yield but, to protect the vines from stress.

Careful vineyard management has been the central focus of Mike Peterkin's efforts as he strives to gain intensity of flavour and full ripeness from his chardonnay grapes. The first vines are now fourteen years old and new vines planted in 1986 were not considered suitable for his Chardonnay until 1993.

The low technology, minimal handling that has become a feature of the way this wine is made has played an equally significant part in the rise to prominence of the Pierro Chardonnay. Since 1986, Mike Peterkin has used a minimal intervention technique: combining knowledge, care and control to make 'low tech' wines. Among other things, this involves using low levels of sulphur, barrel fermentation, lees aging for twelve months, encouraging one hundred per cent malolactic fermentation and maintaining constant temperature control.

The Pierro Chardonnays from 1986 onwards are amazingly consistent from vintage to vintage and all are of outstanding quality. In the Margaret River, only the Leeuwin Estate Art Series Chardonnays can match them.

FORRESTAL FAVOURITE

1991 Chardonnay

This is a subtle, sophisticated wine with hints of melons and peaches and a nutty, almondy character from its charry oak. It is a complex chardonnay which is delicate yet has a depth of rich, concentrated fruit flavour, The wine is supple, lively and persistent with excellent balance and a long, crisp, dry finish complexed by toasty oak and hints of butterscotch.

Caves Road, Willyabrup.
(About one kilometre south of the junction with Metricup Road, on the east side of Caves Road between Palmers and Ribbon Vale.)

Postal address
PO Box 522
BUSSELTON 6280

Phone *(097) 556 220*
Fax   *(097) 556 308*

Hours of opening
10am to 5pm daily

Specialities
Tee shirts

Owners
Mike Peterkin:
with minor shareholders
Bevan Lawrence and
Peter Thompson

Chief Executive / Winemaker
Mike Peterkin

Established
1980

Production
120 tonnes
4,000 cases (1993)
7,000 cases (1994)

Area planted
8.6 ha.

Varieties planted

Chardonnay	4.0 ha.
Chenin Blanc	0.4 ha.
Sauvignon Blanc	1.0 ha.
Cabernet Sauvignon	1.0 ha.
Cabernet Franc/Malbec/ Merlot/Petit Verdot	1.0 ha.
Pinot Noir	1.2 ha.

Wines produced

Pierro Blanc de Blanc A blend of sauvignon blanc and chenin blanc.	*$13.90*
Pierro Chardonnay	*$22.90*
Pierro Pinot Noir	*$17.90*
Pierro Semillon Sauvignon Blanc LTC LTC: this blend of semillon, sauvignon blanc & chardonnay was originally called 'Les Trois Cuvèes'.	*$14.90*
Fire Gully Margaret River Classic A fruity blend of semillon, sauvignon blanc and chenin blanc.	*$11.90*
Fire Gully Cabernets Merlot Cabernet sauvignon, cabernet franc and merlot.	*$13.90*
Fire Gully Pinot Noir	*$11.90*
Fire Gully Late Harvest Chenin	*$10.90*

REDGATE

BILL Ullinger, was born in Carnarvon, a thousand kilometres north of Perth, and worked as an engineer before deciding to turn his hand to producing wine. He purchased land about seven kilometres south of the township of Margaret River within three kilometres of the coast. The winery which he built there was named after the nearby beach off which the Georgette had sunk about a hundred years before.

Planting of the vineyard began in 1977, the first vintage took place in 1981, and another hectare of sauvignon blanc was recently added. Full production of about 150 tonnes should be reached in the near future.

The Cabernet Sauvignon is Redgate's best wine. Its second vintage, the 1982, won the prestigious 1984 Montgomery Trophy at the Adelaide Show, the 1985 and 1988 wines were selected in the Sydney International Top 100 Competition and the most recent vintages, 1991 and 1992, have been very good wines, the latter winning the 1994 SGIO Trophy for best Western Australian cabernet.

I have found many of the reserve wines from Redgate (both red and white) too oaky but that is not the case with the 1991 Cabernet Sauvignon Reserve. This shows intense, coconutty, vanillan oak on the nose and ripe, blackcurrant, fruit on its fleshy mid-palate. It has velvety texture, richness and concentration of flavour and admirable balance.

Redgate have several wines which are for sale but not for tasting. These include the Pinot Noir MC a sparkling wine made by the Methode Champenoise $23.00, the Riesling $10, the Classic Dry White (a blend of sauvignon blanc and semillon) $12, the Cabernet Bin 588, an easy drinking blend of cabernet, cabernet franc and merlot $12.00, the Pinot Noir Reserve $24 and the Botrytis Riesling (for 375ml.) $18.00.

FORRESTAL FAVOURITES

1991 Cabernet Sauvignon
A well-made wine that shows Margaret River's affinity for this variety. It is big and rich with ripe sweet redcurrant and red cherry characters which are well-integrated with charry oak, has a tight structure and firm but fine tannins.

1992 Cabernet Sauvignon
This trophy winner has ripe, red berry, and minty aromas, is clean, fresh and full flavoured and has a firmish finish of good length.

1992 Botrytis Riesling,
A magnificent wine: it has intense, perfumed, apricot and marmalade aromas, is soft and full with rich, concentrated, lush fruit and a long, crisp finish.

Boodjidup Road, Margaret River.
(Turn right off Bussell Highway, 1 km south of the townsite, into Boodjidup Road and follow that road for 6 km.
Off Caves Road, turn into Boodjidup Road. The entrance to the winery is just under one km from the corner.)

Postal address
PO Box 117
MARGARET RIVER 6285

Phone (097) 576 208
Fax   (097) 576 308

Hours of opening
10am to 5pm daily

Specialities
Redgate Wine Suit (made from neoprene wet suit material) $18.50, tee shirts, caps, sweat shirts, waiter's friend corkscrew, Bordex wine racks, ceramic port crock and paintings by local artist, Judith Reynolds.

Owners
Redgate Wines P/L
(Bill, Dorothea and Paul Ullinger)

Chief Executive
Bill Ullinger

Winemakers
Andrew Forsell and Paul Ullinger

Established
1977

Production
200 tonnes
7,500 cases (1993)
8,000 cases (1994)

Area planted
17.9 ha.

Varieties planted

Chardonnay	0.3 ha.
Chenin Blanc	2.7 ha.
Sauvignon Blanc	1.7 ha.
Semillon	2.6 ha.
Riesling	2.6 ha.
Cabernet Franc	1.4 ha.
Cabernet Sauvignon	4.2 ha.
Merlot	0.7 ha.
Pinot Noir	1.5 ha.
Shiraz	0.2 ha.

Wines produced

Redgate Sauvignon Blanc/Semillon	*$10.00*
Redgate Sauvignon Blanc Reserve An oak aged wine.	*$16.50*
Redgate Chardonnay An unwooded chardonnay.	*$16.00*
Redgate Chardonnay Reserve	*$18.00*
Redgate Spatlese Riesling	*$13.00*
Redgate Pinot Noir	*$14.50*
Redgate Cabernet Franc	*$16.00*
Redgate Cabernet Sauvignon	*$16.50*
Redgate White Port	*$13.50*
Redgate Shiraz Port	*$16.50*

RIBBON VALE

JOHN James was an industrial chemist with Midland Brick who enjoyed drinking wine and harboured a desire to make it. When David Gregg gave him a memorable half bottle of the 1972 Vasse Felix Riesling, it triggered an interest in the area and the purchase of land subdivided by the Huttons (of Gralyn) in 1976.

James continued to work for Midland Brick for nine more years, developing Ribbon Vale in his spare time. The block has the most wonderful, sweeping views of the Willyabrup Valley and is only 185 metres wide by 1.3 kilometres long, hence the name. The emblem of the winery is the distinctive blue wren which frequents the vineyard.

The white wines from 1982 to 1988 were made at Cape Mentelle, while the 1982 reds were made by Di Cullen and those from 1983 to 1987 by John James at Willespie. The winery was ready for the 1988 reds and Mike and Jan Davies arrived in time to make those.

The winery caused a sensation at the 1993 Perth Show when its 1993 Sauvignon Blanc won three trophies. It's arguably the best wine of this variety produced in WA.

I doubt if you'll ever be disappointed with a Ribbon Vale white and more often than not you'll be delighted. Both the Semillon and the Sauvignon Blanc are among the best from the region and the Semillon/Sauvignon Blanc is a fine example of this blend.

The Cabernet and Cabernet Merlots are huge, powerful wines that are rich and concentrated with some extraction and firm tannins. They are not for the faint of heart, nor for those unprepared to give them ten years cellaring. The Merlot is consistently first rate: the equal of any from the area.

FORRESTAL FAVOURITES

1993 Sauvignon Blanc
An outstanding white that has powerful aromas of cut grass and gooseberries, as well as richness, concentration and intensity of mid-palate flavour. It has weight that is rare in a wine of this variety and a crisp, clean finish that lingers.

1991 Merlot
An intense red with plum and dark cherry characters, is supple, rich and concentrated with attractive texture, good weight and fine but substantial tannins. With five or so years cellaring, this powerful yet elegant red will mellow and develop a velvety texture but will retain its delicious flavour.

Caves Road, Willyabrup.
(Just over a kilometre south of the
junction with Metricup Road,
between Pierro and Gralyn.)

Postal address
PO Box 127
COWARAMUP 6284

Phone (097) 556 272
Fax   (097) 556 337

Hours of opening
10am to 5pm weekends, public
holidays and all January.

Owner
John James

Chief Executive
John James

Winemaker
Jan and Mike Davies

Established
1977

Production
66 tonnes
3000 cases (1993)
3,500 cases (1994)

Area planted
7.0 ha.

Varieties planted

Chardonnay	0.2 ha.
Sauvignon Blanc	1.7 ha.
Semillon	2.0 ha.
Cabernet Franc	0.2 ha.
Cabernet Sauvignon	1.2 ha.
Merlot	1.7 ha.

Wines produced

Ribbon Vale Estate Semillon	*$10*
Ribbon Vale Semillon	*$12*
Ribbon Vale Oak Matured Semillon	*$12*
Ribbon Vale Sauvignon Blanc	*$14*
Ribbon Vale Sweet Sauvignon Blanc	*$10*
Ribbon Vale Semillon/Sauvignon Blanc	*$12*
Ribbon Vale Cabernet Sauvignon	*$15*
Ribbon Vale Merlot	*$16*
Ribbon Vale Cabernet/Merlot	*$16*

RIVENDELL

PETE and Lu Standish were farmers at Esperance for twenty five years before selling up in 1983 and looking for a lifestyle change in the Margaret River area. They decided to set up a market garden and so developed five hectares at Rivendell between 1983 and 1986. Their produce was sent to Perth and made into preserves there.

In 1985, the Standishes went into partnership with John and Jane Moulden to process a range of preserves on the property. This partnership was dissolved in 1990 with the Mouldens continuing to produce preserves under the Rivendell label.

Meanwhile twelve hectares of vines were planted between 1986 and 1989 with one of the Standish's sons, Mark, taking on responsibility for the vineyard and for overseeing the development of the wine side of the business. The first Rivendell wine, a semillon sauvignon blanc blend was produced in 1990. That, and subsequent wines, have been made by Jan and Mike Davies at Ribbon Vale.

The vineyard was sold in 1990 but has been leased back and the Rivendell wines will continue to be produced. A shiraz from the 1994 vintage will eventually be added to the range. At present, up to ninety per cent of production is sold through cellar door, although some is available in local bottles shops and on the Perth market.

A visit to Rivendell Gardens and Tearooms is invariably a pleasant experience and is warmly recommended. The wines, which are still from young vines, have not yet reached their full potential although those from the 1994 vintage show promise and are very reasonably priced.

FORRESTAL FAVOURITE

1994 Verdelho

This is the best wine I've seen from Rivendell so far: being clean, fresh and well-made with distinct varietal character, perfumed tropical fruit aromas and intense passionfruit flavours. It has a soft, lively mouthfeel, and a crisp dry finish.

Wildwood Road, Yallingup.
(Off Bussell Highway, drive 12 km
along Wildwood Road.)

Postal address
Wildwood Road
YALLINGUP 6282

Phone (097) 552 090
Fax   (097) 552 295

Hours of opening
10am to 5pm daily

Cafe
Open 10am to 5pm daily for lunch,
morning and afternoon teas

Specialities
Tee shirts and a huge range of top
quality jams, chutneys, sauces,
massage oils, creams under the
Rivendell label. An upstairs gallery
often has art exhibitions.

Owners
Pete and Lu Standish

Chief Executive
Mark Standish

Winemaker
Jan and Mike Davies

Viticulturist
Mark Standish

Established
1986

Production
90 tonnes
750 cases (1993)
1300 cases (1994)

Area planted
12.5 ha.

Varieties planted

Cabernet Franc	0.7 ha.
Cabernet Sauvignon	3.6 ha.
Merlot	0.9 ha.
Shiraz	1.5 ha.
Sauvignon Blanc	1.6 ha.
Semillon	2.4 ha.
Verdelho	1.8 ha.

Wines produced

Rivendell Semillon/Sauvignon Blanc	*$10*
Rivendell Verdelho	*$10*
Rivendell Shiraz/Cabernet	*$11*
Rivendell Cabernets Cabernet sauvignon 55%, cabernet franc 25%, merlot 20%.	*$12*
Rivendell Honeysuckle A late harvest semillon.	*$10*
ALSO AVAILABLE	
Moulden's Fragaria A sweet strawberry fruit wine.	*(375ml) $8*

ROSA BROOK

THERE is a novel link with history at Rosa Brook as a careful look at the interior of the tasting cottage will reveal its origin as the Group Settlement Abattoir during the early 1930s.

John and Richard Cooper planted vines during the eighties before subdivided their block and selling off the vineyard to a Perth radiation-oncologist John Shepherd in February 1993.

There has been an amazing turn around in the fortunes of Rosa Brook since the advent of Dan Pannell as winemaker in December 1993. At that time, the vineyard was in need of attention, many of the wines either lacked flavour or were faulty. The better wines were released under the Comfort Hill label while those bearing the winery's name were relegated to what was essentially a second label.

The revitalisation of Rosa Brook has been a major achievement for Pannell, son of Moss Wood founders Bill and Sandra Pannell. All the sub-standard wines were sold off as clean skins so as not to harm the winery's reputation; the Comfort Hill range has been dropped; and new, improved packaging will make the marketing of Rosa Brook easier.

A great deal of work has been done in the vineyard, starting with soil nutrient adjustment and trellising. There has been grafting of varieties which had been planted among other varieties and replanting has taken place where vines had not taken. Some varieties had been planted on unsuitable soil and these vines have been grafted over to more suitable varieties.

Further expansion will see a hectare of each of cabernet sauvignon, cabernet franc and chardonnay planted in 1995 and a further hectare of cabernet sauvignon, plus one each of sauvignon blanc and semillon in 1996, bringing production to 150 tonnes.

The Shepherds have not been afraid to spend money upgrading the winery and investing in new French oak.

The wines of Rosa Brook, which are clean and well-made with good varietal character, are likely to improve with each vintage.

FORRESTAL FAVOURITES

1994 Semillon Sauvignon Blanc
Has attractive, honeysuckle and passionfruit characters with a hint of grassiness, is soft and full flavoured and has a crisp, fresh finish.

1994 Semillon
A finer, more austere style with a hint of capsicum on the mid-palate and a touch of passionfruit on the finish.

Owners
John and Joan Shepherd

Chief Executive
John Shepherd

Winemaker
Dan Pannell

Consultant
Keith Mugford

Established
1986

Production
42 tonnes
1500 cases (1993)
1600 cases (1994)

Area planted
7.1 ha.

Varieties planted

Cabernet Sauvignon	1.6 ha.
Merlot	1.2 ha.
Shiraz	2.1 ha.
Chardonnay	2.0 ha.
Sauvignon Blanc	0.7 ha.
Semillon	1.0 ha.
Riesling	1.0 ha.

Rosa Brook Road
(Turn off Bussell Highway about 2km south of the Margaret River townsite onto Rosa Brook Road. The winery is 2 km down that road.

Postal address
PO Box 366
MARGARET RIVER 6285

Phone (097) 572 286
Fax   (097) 573 634

Hours of opening
11am to 4pm Thurs to Sun during summer.
By appointment only in winter (from end of April school holidays to beginning of October school holidays).

Wines produced

Rosa Brook Chardonnay	*$18.00*
Rosa Brook Semillon Sauvignon Blanc	*$14.00*
Rosa Brook Semillon	*$14.00*
Rosa Brook Cabernet Merlot	*$16.00*
Rosa Brook Merlot	*$14.00*
Rosa Brook Autumn Harvest Riesling	*$12.50*
Rosa Brook Botrytis Riesling	*(375 ml) $14.00*

SANDALFORD

S ANDALFORD can trace its origins back to 1840 when the colony's Surveyor General, John Septimus Roe, was given a land grant of 500 hectares on the upper reaches of the Swan River at Caversham. It was named after the Berkshire priory at which Roe's father was rector. The Roe family maintained an involvement in the winery for just over 150 years until the multi-national conglomerate, Inchape, purchased the family's remaining shares in 1991.

The winery returned to local ownership in 1992 when it was purchased by Peter Prendiville, Paul Naughton and Helen and Steve Palmer. The Prendivilles are now the sole owners.

When Sandalford purchased their Margaret River property in 1970 and planted what is still the state's largest vineyard, they were among the region's pioneers. Like their neighbours, Evans and Tate, Sandalford have their headquarters and winery in the Swan Valley and grapes from Margaret River are transported there for processing.

A failure to maintain adequate investment during the eighties, among other things, lead to the winery and vineyards becoming run down, and, of course, the quality of the wines suffered.

Happily, there has been a gradual but perceptible turnaround since the local buyback. Substantial funds have been invested, the vineyards rejuvenated, the winery modernised and Sandalford's place in the market redefined.

The size of the crush will increase dramatically over the next three years, peaking at about 2,500 tonnes in 1997. Sensibly, the amount produced and marketed under the Sandalford label will increase much more gradually, with the surplus being sold off to finance further investment in new oak and state-of-the-art equipment. Although much remains to be done, the process of revitalisation is well under way and it will not be long before Sandalford is recognised as one of the largest and best of the state's wineries.

Metricup Road, Willyabrup.
(The cellar door outlet is off
Metricup Road about 7 km from
Bussell Highway and just under
3 km from Caves Road)

Postal address
  PO Box 140
  GUILDFORD 6055

Head Office
  Phone   (09) 274 5922
  Fax   (09) 274 2154

Vineyard
  Phone   (097) 556 213
  Fax   (097) 556 284

Hours of opening
  11am to 4pm daily

Specialities
  1989 Sandalford Cabernet
  Sauvignon 375ml and 1992
  Sandalford Cabernet Sauvignon
  (1500ml). Barbecue facilities.

Owners
  Peter and Debra Prendiville

Chief Executive
  Peter Prendiville

Chief Winemaker
  Bill Crapsley

Winemaker
  Andrew Spencer-Wright

Viticulturist
  Ian Davies

Established
  1840
  1972: Margaret River vineyard

Production
  900 tonnes
  35,000 cases (1993)
  50,000 cases (1994)

Area planted
  104.65 ha. at Margaret
  River
  11.25 ha. in the Swan
  Valley
  Sandalford owns major
  vineyards at Willyabrup and
  Caversham and has a long
  term lease of the Landsdale
  Vineyard at Mt Barker.

Varieties planted

	Grown at Margaret River	Grown at Swan Valley	Grown at Mt Barker
Chardonnay	7.27		19.00 ha.
Chenin Blanc	2.33	2.20 ha.	
Riesling	47.66		5.00 ha.
Sauvignon Blanc	2.53		
Semillon	3.39	1.00 ha.	
Verdelho	14.23	1.70 ha.	
Cabernet Franc			1.20 ha.
Cabernet Sauvignon	27.24	4.85	20.00 ha.
Merlot			1.20 ha.
Shiraz		1.50	5.00 ha.

Wine produced

Sandalford 1840 Classic Dry White	*$11.95*
Sandalford 1840 Classic Chardonnay	*$11.95*
Sandalford 1840 Classic Dry Red	*$11.95*
Sandalford Margaret River Riesling	*$11.95*
Sandalford Margaret River Verdelho	*$15.95*
Sandalford Margaret River Cabernet Sauvignon	*$13.70*
Sandalford Margaret River Shiraz	*$13.70*

SANDSTONE

S ANDSTONE is the label of the husband and wife wine-making team of Mike and Jan Davies. It specialises in the production of high quality wines using the varieties which the Davies believe best suit the Margaret River area: semillon and cabernet sauvignon.

Both Jan and Mike are graduates of Roseworthy College. Since then Jan has spent five years working for Tollana in the Eden Valley and one at Wynns in Coonawarra while Mike has been at Tyrells, Chapel Hill and Katnook. They did the 1987 vintage in Bordeaux with Jacques Lurton: Jan at Chateau Bonnet and Mike at Chateau La Louviere.

Jan and Mike Davies accepted an offer to move to the Margaret River at the end of 1987. This involved the two of them working as wine-makers at Cape Clairault, Willespie and Ribbon Vale and gave them the opportunity to make wine under the Sandstone label at Ribbon Vale. After two vintages, it became apparent that Willespie needed a full time winemaker and so John Smith took over that position. When Jan left to start a family, Ian Lewis took on winemaking responsibilities at Clairault once again. The Davies still have a close relationship with John James and work as consultant winemakers to Ribbon Vale.

In addition to this, they work as consultants to several small Margaret River producers and to Aquila Estate which is based at Carbooda, just north of Perth, but sources fruit from Margaret River.

The entrepreneurial side of Mike Davies is best illustrated by his establishment of Portavin, Australia's first mobile bottling and packaging business. In a few short years, the business has expanded so that it now operates five plants (seven by late 1995) in Western Australia, South Australia and Victoria. Portavin bottles wine for forty clients in every region of this state and, I believe, has been responsible for significantly improving the quality of the bottling operations of many small wineries.

The fruit for the Sandstone wines has been brought in from vineyards such as Ribbon Vale and Cape Clairault with which the Davies have had close contact. The semillons show attractive ripe flavours, richness, concentration and depth while the cabernets are full flavoured and powerful but approachable and show good integration of fruit and quality oak.

Sandstone wines are available in limited quantities and most is sold in Sydney, Melbourne and Brisbane.

Owners/Winemakers
Jan and Mike Davies

Established
1988

Production
10 tonnes
500 cases (1993)
650 cases (1994)

Area planted
2 ha.

Variety
Semillon   2 ha.

Caves Road, Willyabrup.
(On the corner of Johnson Road.)

Postal address
CMB
CARBUNUP RIVER 6280

Phone (097) 556 271
Fax   (097) 556 292

*No cellar door. Mail order
available.*

Wines produced *MAIL ORDER PRICES*

Sandstone Semillon	*$19.50*
Sandstone Cabernet Sauvignon	*$19.50*

SERVENTY ORGANIC WINES

LYN Serventy came home from hospital with her first baby, Astrid, and, the next day, had her double brick house blown away around her by Cyclone Tracy. Having survived that catastrophe and lost all their material possessions, Lyn and Peter Serventy decided to rethink their lives. This led to them leaving Darwin and buying land in Margaret River, which they had known from their youth. Their property was too small to be viable for sheep and, after checking with the Agriculture Department, the Serventys found that it was suitable for producing grapes.

Growing up as the son of the ornithologist, Dominic, and nephew of the well-known naturalist and environmentalist, Vincent Serventy, meant that Peter was, from a very young age, concerned about the problems caused by pollution and by the use of chemicals in agriculture.

From the start, the Serventys have been determined to manage an organic vineyard and, in the process, have learnt to overcome problems such as mildew and weevils without recourse to chemicals. One of their aims has been to try to make the vineyard as non-monocultural as possible having a variety of insects living in harmony.

No herbicides or poisonous pesticides are used and compost and other natural products are used as fertilisers. Consequently, Serventy Organic Wines have received a triple A rating from NASAA (the National Association of Sustainable Agriculture of Australia). In addition, their wines are made according to the standards set by the Organic Vignerons Association of Australia. This means that they are low in preservatives and have only a small number of additives.

From the first vintage in 1988 until 1993, the wines were made by Frank Kittler. He will remain as consultant to Peter Serventy who has taken over as winemaker from the 1994 vintage.

FORRESTAL FAVOURITE

1992 Shiraz

This gold medal winner at the Mt Barker Show has some appealing distinctive qualities. It has a perfumed, cracked black pepper character on the nose while the palate, which is somewhat one dimensional, is soft and round with attractive peppery, blackcurranty flavours.

Valley Home Vineyard,
Rocky Road, Witchcliffe.
(Take the Bussell Highway south
from Margaret River. Rocky Road is
13 km from the southern boundary
of the township and 4 km south of
the small town of Witchcliffe. Travel
just under 2 km down Rocky Road,
take the first turn right after the
bitumen ends.)

Postal address
  Post Office
  WITCHCLIFFE 6285

  Phone (097) 577 534
  Fax   (097) 573 541

Hours of opening
  10am to 5pm, Friday, Saturday and
  Sundays.
  Also school and public holidays.

Owners
  Peter and Lyn Serventy

Winemaker
  Peter Serventy

Consultant
  Frank Kittler

Established
  1984

Production
  15 tonnes
  1000 cases (1993)
  1500 cases (1994)

Area planted
  4.0 ha.

Varieties planted

Pinot Noir	1.2 ha.
Shiraz	1.2 ha.
Chardonnay	1.6 ha.

Wines produced

Serventy Sparkling	*§16*
Serventy Chardonnay	*§13*
Serventy Dry White	*§9*
Serventy Dry Red	*§9*
Serventy Pinot Noir	*§13*
Serventy Shiraz	*§13*

THORNHILL

SETTLEMENT on what is now the Berry Farm first took place in 1925. For many years, it was the home of the Vinall family who purchased it using inheritance money from England that came from a property called Thornhill. The Vinalls still have strong emotional ties to the area because of the hardships they experienced during the years spent developing the farm.

In 1976, the 100 hectare farm was bought by Eion and Andrea Lindsay, who came from Victoria to find a new, self-sufficient lifestyle in the Margaret River. They planted kiwi fruit and started a market garden to provide cash flow while waiting for their first saleable crop. The Lindsays also planted avocados, pecan nuts, nashi fruit and some grape vines. As the kiwi fruit came on stream, they scaled back the market garden, except for the berries.

The expansion of the wine industry in the region attracted many visitors and hence a market for value added fruit products. Consequently, in 1985, Eion and Andrea decided to set up the Berry Farm. They started with some jams and twelve months later introduced a range of fruit wines. To show their serious intent, they employed well-respected winemaker, Rob Bowen, as their consultant. As a side line, they developed a range of vinegars which have become an important part of the Berry Farm produce.

The vineyard was planted in 1986 but difficulties with emus and birds, together with the need to concentrate on other parts of the business, delayed the first crop until 1991.

They have used the name Thornhill for their wine label as a tribute to the pioneering work of the Vinall family.

The Lindsays are confident that their wines will eventually make a name for themselves as the Chapman Valley microclimate is quite different from other parts of the Margaret River region. It is much cooler, receives more rain and the grapes ripen later than the more northerly areas. Only small volumes will be produced and most will be sold at the cellar door.

Owners
Eion and Andrea Lindsay

Winemaker
Eion Lindsay

Consultant winemaker
John Smith

Established
1986

Production
124 tonnes
500 cases (1993)
1000 cases (1994)

Area planted
3.6 ha.

Varieties planted
Sauvignon Blanc   1.2 ha.
Semillon   1.2 ha.
Cabernet Sauvignon   1.2 ha.

*The Berry Farm, Bessell Road,
Margaret River.*
(Two km south of the Margaret
River township, turn off Bussell
Highway into Rosa Brook Road.
After 8 km turn right into Rosa Glen
Road and drive another 6 km before
turning left into Bessell Road.)

Postal address
RMB 222, Bessell Road,
MARGARET RIVER 6285

Phone (097) 575 054
Fax   (097) 575 054

Hours of opening
10am to 4.30pm daily

The Berry Farm Cafe
10am to 4.30pm daily

Specialities
Pick your own fruit in season: fresh
produce is available except during
the winter months. The Berry Farm
produces a range of eleven fruit
wines including ones made from
kiwi fruit, plum, pear, boysenberry
as well as raspberry wine,
strawberry, pear, cider, herb,
honey, red and white wine vinegars. In addition, they market more
than twenty jams or conserves and
preserves such as brandy cumquats,
preserved figs, prunes in plum port
and shiraz jelly. All are available for
tasting.

Wines produced

Thornhill Sauvignon Blanc	*$11.50*
Thornhill Classic Dry White 100% semillon.	*$11.50*
Thornhill Cabernet Sauvignon	*$14.00*
Thornhill Pickled Pink A sweet sparkling wine made from cabernet sauvignon.	*$12.00*

TREETON

AVID McGowan spent the first fifteen years of his working life at sea off the Western Australian coast in fishing and charter boats, tugs and dredges before coming ashore at the age of thirty three. He studied as a community recreation officer but ended up teaching navigation and later becoming head of the School of Maritime Studies at the Fremantle Technical College.

Fishing with members of the Portuguese and Italian community sparked an interest in wine which developed into a love affair during a working holiday in Europe in 1971. During this trip, David McGowan travelled through Germany and then picked grapes in Burgundy and Bordeaux. Having become convinced that a vigneron's lot was what he wanted, David looked for land.

In 1982, he found a block which became the Treeton Estate property and worked on it for almost ten years on weekends and during his twelve weeks annual holiday from TAFE (Technical and Further Education). It took a few years to clear and fence the land, get water and build a cabin on the property. The vineyard was then planted in 1986. Because the McGowans were not living on the property, cows got into the vineyard on two occasions and ate most of the vines. The other major difficulty they faced was having to water the vines individually because they had no irrigation system in place. David swears that next time an irrigation plant would be the first priority.

After fifteen years at TAFE, David McGowan took a year's long service leave in 1992 and returned to the fishing industry, skippering a scallops boat at Shark Bay to finance the building and equipping of the winery. During that year, the McGowans moved down to Treeton to live, and since 1993, David has worked as the South West Co-ordinator for TAFE.

Treeton's first vintage, in 1991, was made by Neil Gallagher at Woody Nook: 1500 bottles of shiraz. The second was fermented at Woody Nook but stored in barrel at Treeton and the 1993 vintage was made by Maria Melsom at the humble but new Treeton winery. There were problems with powdery mildew during the 1994 growing season which resulted in the loss of eight tonnes of grapes. Subsequently, a part-time worker has been employed to give greater attention to the vineyard.

Cellar door and mailing list sales have been established and the wines are available in bottle shops and restaurants in the region.

*Lot 1, North Treeton Road,
Cowaramup.*
*(Look for the signpost on Bussell
Highway just north of the township
of Cowaramup, travel 2km along
Treeton Road and turn left. The
winery is a little more than a
kilometre along the narrow,
winding North Treeton Road.)*

Owners
David and Corinne McGowan

Chief executive
David McGowan

Winemaker
Maria Melsom

Established
1986

Production
10 tonnes
1200 cases (1993)
1200 cases (1994)

Area planted
5.0 ha.

Varieties planted

Shiraz	2.5 ha.
Chardonnay	1.5 ha.
Semillon	1.0 ha.

Postal address
PO Box 219
COWARAMUP 6284

Phone (097) 555 481
Fax (097) 555 051

Hours of opening
Daily 10 am to 6pm

Specialities
Self serve nibbles

Wines produced

Treeton Estate Chardonnay	*$15.00*
Treeton Estate Semillon	*$12.50*
Treeton Estate Cabernet Sauvignon	*$15.00*
Treeton Estate Petit Rouge A sweet blush made from shiraz.	*$13.00*
Treeton Estate Shiraz	*$14.00*
Treeton Estate Port Made from shiraz.	*$13.00*

VASSE FELIX

WHEN Dr Tom Cullity planted his vineyard in 1967 he was the first to react to John Gladstones's research papers which suggested that the area was particularly suited to the production of premium wines. Cullity named the winery after the French seaman on the Geographe who lost his life when a longboat overturned at the mouth of the river which now bears his name.

As the first vineyard in the area, Vasse Felix suffered severe bird damage and Cullity attempted to scare the birds away with trained falcons. The perigrine falcon has become the striking emblem of the winery in spite of its failure to return once allowed free flight.

David Gregg became winemaker in 1973 and Cullity sold the winery to him in 1984. The Greggs sold to the Holmes à Courts in 1987 and David Gregg accepted a position as manager. An initial three year contract was extended to five, after which he chose to retire.

The winery has continued to flourish under the Holmes à Court ownership. The South-West's oldest vineyard, Forest Hill at Mount Barker, was purchased in 1989. Long term access to this high quality fruit has been retained in spite of the property being sold in 1993. There has been increased spending on new oak and expensive winemaking equipment and a further 10 hectares of semillon, shiraz and merlot has been planted at Margaret River.

In recent times, the Vasse Felix Shiraz has been outstanding and I regard it as one of the benchmarks for the variety in Western Australia. In great vintages like 1988, 1990, 1991 and 1993, it ranks among the best in Australia. Apart from the powerful fruit from old vines, the major influence on the style has been the use of oak: 20% is barrel fermented in new American oak and the wine is aged for twelve months in new oak: 80% American and 20% French.

Vasse Felix has always been among the first rank of the region's wineries and has produced many outstanding wines: none better than the 1979 and 1985 Cabernets, two of the best red wines ever produced in the Margaret River.

FORRESTAL FAVOURITE

1993 Shiraz
Both the 1990 and 1991 Vasse Felix Shiraz were stunning, intense, complex wines with show records to match. The 1993 Vasse Felix Shiraz is a powerful, dense red that has good weight, a silky texture, rich, concentrated, spicy vanillan oak and blackberry characters and a long, dry finish. It is approachable now but will improve with medium term cellaring and is worth every cent of its price tag.

Caves Road, Willyabrup.
(Situated on the corner of Caves Road and Harmans Road South.)

Postal address:
PO Box 32
COWARAMUP 6285

Phone	(097) 555 242
Fax	(097) 555 425

Hours of opening
10am to 4pm daily

Cafe
10am to 4pm daily, lunch, morning and afternoon teas.

Owners
Heytesbury Holdings
(Janet Holmes à Court and family)

Chief Executive
Bob Baker

Winemaker:
Clive Otto

Production manager:
Bruce Pearse

Established
1967

Production
400 tonnes
20,000 cases (1993)
30,000 cases (1994)

Area planted	Margaret River	Mount Barker
	9 ha.	25 ha.

Varieties planted	Margaret River	Mount Barker
Chardonnay		6.0 ha.
Riesling	2.0 ha.	6.8 ha.
Sauvignon Blanc		1.2 ha.
Verdelho	1.0 ha.	
Cabernet Sauvignon	4.0 ha.	8.0 ha.
Malbec	1.0 ha.	
Shiraz	1.0 ha.	3.0 ha.

Wines produced

Vasse Felix Non-vintage Brut	*$30.00*
Vasse Felix Chardonnay From the Forest Hill Vineyard.	*$22.00*
Vasse Felix Theatre White A blend of verdelho, riesling and traminer.	*$10.00*
Vasse Felix Classic Dry White	*$17.50*
Vasse Felix Theatre Dry Red In 1993, a blend of cabernet sauvignon, cabernet franc and merlot.	*$10.00*
Vasse Felix Classic Dry Red	*$17.50*
Vasse Felix Cabernet Sauvignon	*$24.00*
Vasse Felix Shiraz	*$24.50*
Vasse Felix Noble Riesling From the Forest Hill Vineyard.	(375ml) *$19.00*

VASSE RIVER

THE Cedaro family have been farming this property since 1922, firstly specialising in dairy production and growing potatoes but more recently the 400 hectare farm has been used for sheep and cattle. Albert continued a tradition begun by his father who planted a few vines to produce wine for family use. He had planted the Italian red varietal, fragola, which had been grown by the Meleri family in their Yallingup vineyard since 1915.

More than twenty years ago, Bill Pannell had encouraged Albert to plant more vines but he decided against it because of the expense involved. However, on retiring from farming, Albert decided to expand his vineyard and to build a winery. With his son, Robert, he planted an initial six hectares and an additional fourteen hectares in 1993.

This latter expansion has meant that the vineyard has become more than a retirement project for Albert and Ruby and so Robert and Phyllis have become involved. The vineyard and winery has enabled the Cedaros to diversify their farming interests. Much of the production is sold off as grapes. The wine is sold mainly through the cellar door.

The first vintage was made under contract at Moss Brothers and labelled Carbunup Estate. The second vintage was made at the new winery by Maria Melsom and was released either as Carbunup Estate or Vasse River Wines. This latter label was developed with the retail market in mind, as the Cedaros have decided to sell small quantities of the wine in Perth. Understandable confusion arose from the presence of two labels and from 1994 the wines will be released as Vasse River.

A rare gold medal and praise from the judges for the 1993 Vasse River Chardonnay at the Perth Show following a silver medal in Mount Barker has given the winery's reputation a timely boost.

FORRESTAL FAVOURITES

1993 Chardonnay
This wine is soft, clean and fresh with grassy, figgy flavours and a touch of spiciness.

1992 Cabernet Sauvignon
Shows promise of better things to come with some dark cherry and plummy fruit characters but is quite lean on the mid-palate and is astringent and very dry on the finish. Older vines and better oak will see this promise fulfilled.

Bussell Highway, Carbunup.
(Situated on the main highway, just 3 kilometres south of the small township of Carbunup.)

Postal address
Post Office
CARBUNUP RIVER 6280

Phone (097) 551 163
Fax   (097) 551 111

Hours of opening
10am to 5pm daily

Owners
Albert and Ruby,
Robert and Phyllis Cedaro

Chief Executive
Robert Cedaro

Winemaker
Peter Stark

Consultant
John Smith

Established
1989

Production
40 tonnes
900 cases (1993)
1050 cases (1994)

Area planted
20.0 ha.

Varieties planted

Chardonnay	8.0 ha.
Semillon	4.0 ha.
Verdelho	1.5 ha.
Cabernet Sauvignon	4.0 ha.
Merlot	1.0 ha.
Shiraz	1.5 ha.

Wines produced

Vasse River Chardonnay	*$12.50*
Vasse River Semillon	*$9.00*
Vasse River Cabernet Sauvignon	*$12.50*
Carbunup Estate Cabernet Sauvignon	*$12.00*
Carbunup Estate Cabernet Merlot	*$12.00*
Carbunup Estate Verdelho A late picked sweet white.	*$11.00*
Carbunup Estate Port Made from shiraz.	*$13.00*

VIRAGE

THE Bramley Estate Vineyard was planted in 1975 as the Government Research Station to test the viability of the region for viticulture. Bernard and Pascale Abbott were particularly attracted by the opportunity of obtaining a long term lease on the vineyard because of the quality of its cabernet and because it offered Virage the luxury of producing wine from mature vines from the outset.

Originally from the Clare Valley, Bernard Abbott is a Roseworthy graduate who worked for three years as winemaker at Vasse Felix and has done vintage at Petaluma, Leasingham, at Chateau Chevalier in the Napa, at Pommery in Champagne, at Chateau Bonnet in Bordeaux as well as spending two vintages working in the Rheingau. Pascale, who was born in Marseille, has worked in cellar door sales at three Margaret River wineries.

The Abbotts produce and distribute Virage wines. It is their understanding of the industry which has enabled them to do this successfully with limited capital expenditure.

They believe that there is a niche in the market for a small family business in which the winemaker is in direct contact with the retailer. In addition, they take every opportunity to obtain feedback from the public about their wines. Most of the Virage wines are sold through fine wine retailers in Perth and small amounts are sold in Melbourne and Sydney.

Two more hectares of cabernet, semillon and sauvignon blanc have been planted and will come into production in 1997, thus enabling Virage to expand its capacity.

FORRESTAL FAVOURITES

1991 Cabernet Sauvignon
Includes some merlot (8%) in the blend and is a medium bodied wine which is soft and approachable with some lifted, blackcurrant characters, a touch of new oak and some sweet tannins. This well-made Margaret River red is flavoursome, reasonably priced and good current drinking.

1992 Cabernet Nouveau
This is a fruit driven wine which has been aged in one year old oak. It is a good quaffing wine with an attractive herbal nose and pleasant mid-palate flavour.

Bramley Estate, Bussell Highway, Cowaramup
(There are no signs on the vineyard which is situated about 6km north of Margaret River. If you are heading from Cowaramup to Margaret River, the vineyard is on your left about 100 metres past Burnside Road, which goes off Bussell Highway to your right.)

Postal address
PO Box 220
COWARAMUP 6284

Phone (097) 555 318
Fax   (097) 555 318

Visits by appointment only.

Owners
Bernard and Pascale Abbott

Winemaker
Bernard Abbott

Established
1990

Production
30 tonnes
1400 cases (1993)
1800 cases (1994)

Area planted
2.4 ha.

Varieties planted

Chardonnay	400 vines
Chenin Blanc	100 vines
Colombard	100 vines
Riesling	200 vines
Sauvignon Blanc	200 vines
Semillon	200 vines
Sylvanner	100 vines
Traminer	100 vines
Verdelho	100 vines
Cabernet Franc	100 vines
Cabernet Sauvignon	1.2 ha.
Merlot	100 vines
Petit Verdot	100 vines
Pinot Meunier	100 vines
Pinot Noir	100 vines
Shiraz	100 vines
Zinfandel	100 vines

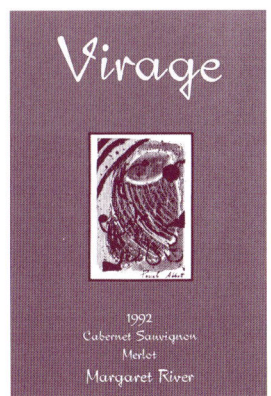

Wines produced

Virage Sauvignon Blanc	*$14.00*
Virage Semillon Sauvignon Blanc Chardonnay	*$12.50*
Virage Traminer Riesling A sweet fruity blend of traminer and sylvanner.	*$10.00*
Virage Cabernet Merlot	*$16.00*
Virage Cabernet Shiraz Zinfandel	*$12.00*

VOYAGER

THE wines of Voyager Estate have shown a quantum leap in quality thanks to the substantial investment of owner, Michael Wright and the winemaking talents of Stuart Pym. Wright's family fortune was made from iron-ore exploration in the Pilbara where his father, Peter, was Lang Hancock's partner. Although a tee-totaller, Michael Wright decided to invest in the wine industry and purchased Freycinet Estate from Peter and Jennifer Gheradi in May 1991.

The vineyard is now producing excellent fruit from mature, fifteen year old vines. It is being picked later and riper than before. New trellising has been introduced and all vines are now irrigated. Investment has also been made in first class French oak and state-of-the-art winery equipment which has helped the production of fresh, ultra-clean white wines.

In the 1994 Sheraton Awards, the 1993 Chardonnay was joint winner of the gold medal. A trophy at the Mt Barker Show provided further proof of the wine's quality.

Although the Chardonnay is the best of the Voyager wines, all their whites show pristine cleanliness, intense flavours and distinct varietal character and all are attractively priced and highly recommended.

There is no question in my mind that Voyager is a force to be reckoned with in the Margaret River. A magnificent Cape Dutch building is to be fitted out as a tasting centre and will be among the most impressive in the region.

FORRESTAL FAVOURITES

1993 Chardonnay
This has pristine cleanliness, some complexity, an attractive texture and rich and powerful melon and toasty oak flavours.

1993 Estate Classic
Has pungent, herbal characters with overtones of capsicum, is soft yet full flavoured with a long, grassy finish. It is a clean, well-made wine which has good weight, a tight structure and crisp acidity.

1993 Semillon
Has a small amount of sauvignon blanc (12%) added to give it lift. The wine shows intense, herbal, asparagus and spicy oak characters, is clean and fresh, with complexity and depth of flavour from its oak maturation.

1992 Cabernet Merlot
This sensational red has intense, spicy cassis and charry oak flavours, is soft, round and fleshy It has great richness and concentration and is elegant and well-balanced.

Stevens Road, Margaret River.
(Turn off Bussell Highway 4km
south of Margaret River onto
Gnaraway Road, follow it for just
over 3 km before turning left into
Stevens Road.
From Caves Road, drive 3 km down
Boodjidup Road, turn into
Gnaraway Road and almost
immediately into Stevens Road.)

Postal address
PO Box 102
MOSMAN PARK 6012

Winery
Phone (097) 576 358

Head Office
Phone (09) 385 3133
Fax   (09) 383 4029

The cellar door will open in late
1995.

Owner
Michael Wright

Chief Executive
Michael Wright

Winemaker
Stuart Pym

Consultant
Gary Baldwin

Viticulturist
Michael Melsom

Consultant
Di Davidson

When established
1978 (as Freycinet Estate)

Production
100 tonnes (80 tonne brought in)
3,200 cases (1993)
8,000 cases (1994)

Area planted
20.1 ha.

Varieties planted

Chardonnay	6.8 ha.
Chenin Blanc	2.8 ha.
Sauvignon Blanc	3.3 ha.
Semillon	3.3 ha.
Cabernet Franc	0.2 ha.
Cabernet Sauvignon	2.4 ha.
Merlot	0.8 ha.
Petit Verdot	0.5 ha.

Wines produced

Voyager Estate Chardonnay	*$19.00*
Voyager Estate Chenin Blanc	*$11.50*
Voyager Estate Classic White A blend of semillon & sauvignon blanc 50:50.	*$13.00*
Voyager Estate Semillon	*$16.00*
Voyager Estate Cabernet Merlot	*$19.00*

WILDWOOD

ILDWOOD is a major tourist facility for the Yallingup area which consists of a mud brick winery / restaurant complex with an art gallery attached and chalet accommodation available in four cottages on the property. Approval has been given for another eighteen.

Geoff Eastaugh is an energetic and controversial personality who is a vigorous proponent of the development lobby in the district and, consequently, has been at odds with the wine industry establishment over the years.

He had previously worked in the meat export business before moving to Margaret River with his family. After about five years of farming, he decided to become involved in viticulture and worked as a sub-contractor planting vineyards in the region. At the same time, Geoff and his wife, Lyn, planted their own vineyard. Because of the other work in which they were involved, this took six years to complete.

The first harvest from the vineyard was in 1988 and all wines so far have been made at Redgate. While the vines are young, they have appeared under the second label, Wyadup Brook. Geoff Eastaugh describes these as fun wines designed to appeal to young people. From the 1994 vintage, the wines will appear under the Wildwood label and from 1995 the wines will be made at Wildwood by Geoff and his son, Damon, who is a qualified chemist.

The Eastaughs wish to sell only through the cellar door and on a mailing list. Any surplus fruit that the vineyard produces will be sold off.

Caves Road, Yallingup
(Situated 5km from the Yallingup turn-off.)

Postal address
Post Office
YALLINGUP 6282

Phone: (097) 552 066
Fax: (097) 541 389

Hours of opening
9.30am to late

Restaurant
Open 9.30am until late daily for lunch, dinner, morning and afternoon teas.

Specialities
Cottages for rent, art gallery.

Owners
Geoff and Lyn Eastaugh

Chief Executive
Geoff Eastaugh

Winemaker
Damon Eastaugh

Established
1985

Production
32 tonnes
800 cases (1993)
2000 cases (1994)

Hectares
6.5 ha.

Varieties planted

Chardonnay	1.0 ha.
Chenin Blanc	0.6 ha.
Sauvignon Blanc	0.8 ha.
Semillon	1.2 ha.
Cabernet Franc	0.4 ha.
Cabernet Sauvignon	0.8 ha.
Merlot	0.4 ha.
Pinot Noir	1.2 ha.
Gamay	0.1 ha.

Wines produced

Wildwood Pinot Noir Brut Pink and a touch sweet.	*$20*
Wildwood Chardonnay	*$20*
Wildwood Chenin Blanc A semi sweet wine.	*$16*
Wildwood Semillon	*$15*
Wyadup Caberet Cabernet A semi sweet rose style.	*$15*
Wildwood Cabernet Sauvignon	*$20*
Wildwood Pinot Noir	*$18*
Wyadup Wild Roses A light, fruity, semi sweet blend of pinot & cabernet.	*$15*
Wildwood Honey Dew A sweet blend of chenin blanc and semillon.	*$15*
Wyadup Tawny Port	*$17*

WILLESPIE

TWO years on Cocos Island in 1969-70 gave Kevin and Marian Squance the opportunity to save enough to buy a small farm. While they taught at Brunswick Junction, they looked around the Margaret River region for a suitable block of land.

The Squances found the right property in 1976, and Kevin's interest in growing things was given immediate expression in viticulture. They planted a nursery in 1976 and the vineyard the following year. As part of the second wave of vignerons in the region, the Squances were able to draw on the experience of the pioneers. They decided to plant cabernet and riesling but also planted the less fashionable varieties, verdelho and semillon, which have become the cornerstone of their success.

Kevin Squance was principal of the Margaret River Primary School until he resigned to concentrate on the vineyard and winery in 1987. Marian, an art and craft specialist, at the same school resigned in 1990 after Kevin had suffered a heart attack.

Willespie wines have done well in shows, notably the 1987 Cabernet and the 1990 Sauvignon Blanc which won gold medals in the Sheraton Awards, the 1988 Verdelho winner of a gold at the Mt Barker Show and the 1991 and 1993 Sauvignon Blanc both of which won trophies at the *Winewise* Small Winemakers Awards.

The most impressive of the Willespie wines are the Sauvignon Blanc and the Semillon Sauvignon Blanc blend, both of which are among the best produced in the region. The Sauvignon Blanc tends to be in the herbal rather than tropical fruit spectrum, showing intense green bean and asparagus characters, lively acidity and clean, crisp, fresh flavours.

FORRESTAL FAVOURITES

1993 Semillon/Sauvignon Blanc
Shows pungent, herbaceous aromas and grassy, asparagus characters with a touch of toasty oak on the palate. It is a big wine which is clean, fresh and full of flavour with a crisp, dry finish. A silver medal winner at the Sheraton Awards.

1993 Verdelho
A full flavoured wine with intense passionfruit and guava characters, crisp acidity and a lingering finish.

Harmans Mill Road, Willyabrup.
(From Caves Road, turn down
Metricup Road and right into
Harmans Mill Road. Willespie is the
first winery after the junction.
Off Bussell Highway, take Harmans
Mill Road for just over 5 km.)

Postal address
   RSM 394
   BUSSELTON 6280

   Phone   (097) 556 248
   Fax   (097) 556 210

Hours of opening
   10.30am to 5pm daily.

Specialities
   Cellar door and mail order only

   1990 Willespie Semillon
   (375ml)   *$8.00*

   1990 Willespie Verdelho
   (375ml)   *$8.00*

   1989 Willespie Cabernet
   Sauvignon (375ml)   *$10.50*

   Willespie Merlot   *$22.50*

   Willespie White Port
   Made from verdelho
   (375ml)   *$10.00*

Owners
   Marian and Kevin Squance

Chief Executive
   Marian Squance

Winemaker
   Michael Lemmes

Viticulturist
   Kevin Squance

Established
   1976

Production
   70.1 tonnes
   3800 cases (1993)
   4200 cases (1994)

Area planted
   10.0 ha.

Varieties planted

Sauvignon Blanc	0.8 ha.
Semillon	2.0 ha.
Riesling	1.5 ha.
Verdelho	3.2 ha.
Cabernet Sauvignon	2.2 ha.
Merlot	0.3 ha.

Wines produced

Willespie Rhine Riesling	*$14.00*
Willespie Sauvignon Blanc	*$14.00*
Willespie Semillon Sauvignon Blanc	*$14.00*
Willespie Verdelho	*$14.50*
Willespie Cabernet Sauvignon	*$18.50*
Willespie Late Harvest Rhine Riesling	*$11.00*
Willespie Vintage Port Made from cabernet sauvignon.	*$16.50*
Willespie Harman's Mill White A blend of verdelho 66%, riesling and semillon.	*$10.00*
Willespie Harman's Mill Red A light, fruity, unwooded cabernet sauvignon.	*$11.00*
Willespie Harman's Mill Autumn Whim A sweet pink made from cabernet.	*$10.00*

WISE

AFTER reading John Gladstones's research, entrepreneur, Ron Wise, became convinced that the best properties in the region were close to the ocean and felt that Cape Naturaliste would be an ideal environment for growing grapes, as long as the vineyard land was protected from the wind.

In 1992, Ron and Sandra Wise purchased Geographe Estate and shortly after nearby Eagle Bay Estate. There were several reasons for this: the vineyard had some good eight year old sauvignon blanc and semillon vines as well as some promising shiraz and merlot; the spring provided permanent water sufficient for the two properties and the winery and there was an abundance of gravel - useful for development.

Wise Wines also have interests outside the Margaret River region. The Newlands property at Donnybrook was acquired by Ron Wise in partnership with his friends, Graham Taylor and Gerry Lawrance, and a significant amount of fruit is sourced from the Phoenicia Vineyard at Pemberton. For ease of marketing, all wines will be released under the Wise label. Some regional varietals will be produced but, for the most part, grapes from the different vineyards will be blended.

Although it's early days, I've seen some very pleasant wines from the Wise winery: I particularly like the Merlot and Pinot Noir from Meelup, a 1993 Sauvignon Blanc from Newlands which had the wonderful aromas of granny smith apples and the 1992 Wise Aquercus ('unwooded') Chardonnay.

However, there is much work to be done, both in the vineyard and the winery, before all of the wines are up to their own very high standards. Knowing the calibre of the team and Ron Wise's determination and financial resources, I have no doubt that this challenge will be met.

FORRESTAL FAVOURITES

1993 Pinot Noir
Made from Meelup fruit, this is a delicious, uncomplicated, light bodied red. It has soft, spicy, strawberry characters that is drinking beautifully.

1993 Merlot
Also drinking well is the medium bodied Merlot, which is the best variety being produced at Meelup. It has spicy, plummy characters with a hint of pepper, is supple, round and quite rich and finishes with substantial but soft tannins.

Owners
Ron and Sandra Wise

General Manager
Tim Wise

Winemaker
Mark Ravenscroft

Consultant
Candy Jonsson

Established
1992

Production
50 tonnes
2500 cases (1993)
3000 cases (1994)

Area planted
8.0 ha. at Meelup.
10.3 ha. on the Newlands Vineyard
at Donnybrook.

Varieties planted

Chardonnay	1.1 ha.
Chenin Blanc	0.3 ha.
Sauvignon Blanc	0.2 ha.
Semillon	2.8 ha.
Cabernet Sauvignon	1.6 ha.
Merlot	0.8 ha.
Pinot Noir	0.4 ha.
Shiraz	0.8 ha.

Eagle Bay Road, Meelup.
(From Dunsborough township, take the Naturaliste Road about 5km and take the turn off at Eagle Bay Road to the Vineyard Cafe where tastings of Wise Wines are held.)

Postal address
PO Box 162
DUNSBOROUGH 6281

Winery
Phone (097) 568 098
Fax   (097) 553 979

Head Office
Phone (09) 322 4144
Fax   (09) 322 5918

Hours of opening
Daily 10.30 am to 4pm

Cafe
Lunch Wed to Sun, 11 to 4pm
Dinner Fri to Sat from 6pm.
In summer, dinner also on Thurs.
On long weekends, also dinner
Sunday and lunch Monday.

Specialities
tee shirts, corkscrews and some
paintings for sale.

Wines produced

Wise Sauvignon Blanc Semillon	*$14.50*
Wise Chardonnay	*$18.50*
Wise Classic Dry White Made from semillon.	*$12.00*
Wise Pinot Noir	*$16.50*
Wise Classic Soft Red Made from shiraz.	*$12.00*
Wise Cabernet Sauvignon	*$16.00*
Wise Late Harvest Made mainly from semillon.	*$12.00*

WOODLANDS

DAVID Watson has been a Perth based consulting engineer for 24 years and Heather Watson a lawyer practising in Midland. Woodlands has been a part time passion for them for more than twenty years devouring much of their spare time.

A judge at the Perth Show, David Watson first became interested in wine and winemaking through a family connection with legendary Houghton winemaker, Jack Mann.

He and Heather bought the Woodlands property during a holiday in Busselton in 1973 and established the vineyard with cuttings and advice from Bill Pannell at nearby Moss Wood. David learnt about winemaking in discussions with Jack Mann, through his friendship with David Gregg nurtured during three vintages at Vasse Felix and by reading widely.

From the difficult 1986 vintage until 1991 the Watsons sold off most of their fruit as they reassessed their position. Their equipment was in need of renewal, they were exhausted by their intensive and long term commitment and needed the opportunity to stand back and reflect on what they had done and what they could hope to achieve.

In 1992, the Watsons decided that they would upgrade the vineyard and the winery and rebuild their position in the marketplace. The appointment of viticulturist, Barry Thompson, to work on the property full time has made a significant difference.

The Watsons believe that the influence of viticultural consultant, Richard Smart, and especially changes they've made to trellising will significantly improve their wines by 1995. As well as this, they have acquired a new crusher, new tanks, a red fermenter and a hydraulic press to enable the winery to operate more efficiently.

The best of the wines from this vineyard is the Cabernet Sauvignon with the 1981 vintage producing one of the greatest red wines ever from the Margaret River region.

FORRESTAL FAVOURITES

1991 Cabernet
Of the wines I've seen from Woodlands recently, my favourite has been the 1991 Cabernets which has rich, ripe red berry, red cherry and plummy characters, good mid-palate richness and concentration and some complexity from bottle age.

1989 Emily
The Emily has good weight, is soft and full flavoured with some attractive vanillan oak and rich berry fruit.

Owners
David and Heather Watson

Chief Executive
David Watson

Winemaker
David Watson

Viticulturist
Barry Thompson

Established
1973

Production
17 tonnes
1000 cases (1993)
1500 cases (1994)

Area planted
4.8 ha.

Varieties planted

Chardonnay	0.8 ha.
Cabernet Franc	0.2 ha.
Cabernet Sauvignon	3.0 ha.
Malbec	0.2 ha.
Merlot	0.4 ha.
Pinot Noir	0.2 ha.

Caves Road, Willyabrup.
(The entrance to the winery is on the west side of Caves Road, about 50 metres south of the junction with Metricup Road.)

Postal address
29 Spring Park Road
MIDLAND 6056

Winery
Phone (097) 556 226

Head Office
Phone (09) 274 6155

Visits on weekends, by appointment only.

Wines produced

Woodlands Chardonnay	*$23.00*
Woodlands Cabernet Sauvignon	*$23.00*
MAILING LIST AND RESTAURANTS ONLY	
Woodlands Sauvignon Blanc	*$14.00*
Woodlands 'Emily' Cabernet Sauvignon, A St Emilion blend (hence Emily) of cabernet sauvignon, merlot, malbec, & cabernet franc.	*$12.50*
Woodlands Cabernet Merlot Cabernet sauvignon 66%, merlot 33%.	*$14.00*
Woodlands Pinot Noir A light bodied, early drinking style.	*$18.00*

WOODY NOOK

JEFF and Wynn Gallagher bought twenty eight hectares on Metricup Road in 1978 and moved into the area and semi retirement in 1979. After a few years working on other vineyards, Jeff decided that it was about time he did something with his land and the obvious thing seemed to be to plant vines.

To help out, his son Neil and daughter-in-law Linda, came to live in Margaret River. Neil had spent seventeen years laying carpets and took up a range of labouring jobs (floor tiling, roof plumbing, carpet laying and portable saw milling) for six years so that he could spend the weekends planting the Woody Nook vineyards. As well as this, he built the house and later the winery.

The first vintage, 1987, was experimental and small as bird damage had significantly reduced the crop. The 1988 vintage was made by Jan and Mike Davies at Woody Nook. John Smith made the 1989 wines with Neil Gallagher helping and the following year Neil made wine with John Smith consulting. Since 1991, Neil has made the wines.

About fifty per cent of production is sold through the cellar door. The best of the Woody Nook wines is the Cabernet Sauvignon. The 1990 vintage won the trophy for best Western Australian dry red at the Perth Show and the 1992 vintage a gold medal in the 1994 *Winewise* Small Winemakers Competition.

Metricup Road, Willyabrup.
(Turn off Bussell Highway into
Metricup Road and travel 5km to
the entrance.)

Postal address
RSM 395
BUSSELTON 6280

Phone (097) 557 547
Fax   (097) 557 547

Hours of opening
10am to 4.30pm daily

Cafe
Light lunch, morning and afternoon
teas.

Specialities
Pottery, art, sweatshirts, tee shirts,
port sippers and Wynn Gallagher's
pottery including the popular
Woody Nook pigs

Owners
The Gallagher family

Chief Executive
Linda Gallagher

Winemaker
Neil Gallagher

Established
1979

Production
30 tonnes
1500 cases (1993)
1000 cases (1994)

Area planted
8.1 ha.

Varieties planted

Chardonnay	0.1 ha.
Chenin Blanc	1.0 ha.
Sauvignon Blanc	0.8 ha.
Semillon	1.6 ha.
Verdelho	0.1 ha.
Cabernet Franc	0.1 ha.
Cabernet Sauvignon	2.4 ha.
Merlot	0.4 ha.
Shiraz	1.6 ha.

Wines produced

Woody Nook Chenin Blanc	$11.50
Woody Nook Classic Dry White	$14.50
Woody Nook Sauvignon Blanc	$13.00
Woody Nook Semillon Wood Matured	$14.50
Woody Nook Semillon Sauvignon Blanc	$9.00
Woody Nook Cabernet Sauvignon	$16.00
Woody Nook Merlot	$15.00
Woody Nook Late Harvest Semillon	$13.00
Woody Nook Nooky Delight	$14.50

WRIGHTS

MAUREEN and Henry Wright decided to come to Australia when Henry's job with the British Colonial Office became redundant after Kenya had gained independence. They chose not to go to Maureen's homeland, South Africa, to avoid being in the same position when majority rule came to that country. Western Australia appealed as an exciting prospect and it was the closest English speaking country.

The Wrights had no firm idea of what they wanted to do other than they were committed to agriculture. They worked on a farm in Katanning and then bought a pig farm near Cowaramup. Eventually, the idea of knocking off at 5 o'clock became so appealing that they purchased their current property as a place to live.

Maureen and Henry had long shared an interest in wine and living opposite Vasse Felix, and in an area excited by the first stirrings of the wine industry, decided to sell their other farm and plant vines on the Willyabrup property. In 1977, they realised that selling grapes would not bring an adequate return and decided to make their own wine.

The first commercial vintage was produced in 1979 with two reds and a riesling. The Wrights made their first port in 1981 and over the next twelve vintages produced a series which featured historical houses from the Busselton-Margaret River area. A fire destroyed most of the grapes for the 1993 port but a twenty-first anniversary port will be produced from the 1994 vintage.

In 1982, Henry Wright made what he believes was the first white port in the district from riesling. It has been very successful and has achieved a loyal following. They also produce one barrel of Chardonnay White Port per year which they believe is a unique style. When Southeby's recently auctioned wines from the Czar Nicholas II's cellar for the Russian government, a Swiss collector paid a substantial sum for a hundred year old white port made from chardonnay. He has responded enthusiastically to the Wrights sending him a bottle of their Chardonnay White Port as well as inviting them to visit him at the first opportunity.

The Wright have chosen to keep their operation small and most of their sales are made through the cellar door.

Harmans Mill Road, Willyabrup.
(About one km from the junction of
Caves Road, opposite Vasse Felix.)

Postal address
PO Box 25
COWARAMUP 6284

Phone (097) 555 314
Fax   (097) 555 459

Hours of opening
10am to 4.30 pm daily

Owners
Henry and Maureen Wright

Winemaker
Henry Wright

Established
1973

Production
60 tonnes
1500 cases (1993)
1500 cases (1994)

Area planted
11.8 ha.

Varieties planted

Chardonnay	0.2 ha.
Semillon	2.0 ha.
Riesling	2.8 ha.
Cabernet Sauvignon	3.2 ha.
Shiraz	3.6 ha.

Wines produced

Wrights Premium Estate	*$13.50*
A dry white table wine made from semillon 60% and riesling 40%.	
Wrights White Hermitage	*$13.50*
A lightly wooded, dry white made from shiraz.	
Wrights Hermitage	*$13.50*
Wrights Hermitage/Cabernet Sauvignon	*$13.50*
Wrights Cabernet Sauvignon/Hermitage	*$13.50*
Wrights White Port A sweet fortified wine made from riesling.	*$16.00*
Wrights Chardonnay White Port	*$25.00*
A fortified dessert wine made from chardonnay. Only one barrel is produced each year.	
Wrights Vintage Port A fortified wine made from shiraz.	*$16.00*

XANADU

DR John Lagan and Dr Eithne Sheridan, left the Troubles of Northern Ireland in 1968 to settle in the Margaret River area and work as GPs. They were influenced by their medical colleagues, to plant vines in 1977.

The winery was named after the summer palace of the Chinese emperor in Coleridge's poem, 'Kubla Khan'. There Xanadu is a lush and fertile place, albeit with a shadowy side. The Lagans see it as a sunny place where it is possible to drink 'the milk of Paradise'.

John Smith (winemaker from 1984 to 1989) established Xanadu's reputation as a producer of outstanding chardonnays and excellent wood matured semillons.

The Lagan's son, Conor, returned from Roseworthy in 1989 and was joined by Jürg Muggli, a Swiss viticulturist, winemaker and chef. Lagan and Muggli are confident and brash enough to resist following current trends, but enthusiastic, committed and knowledgeable enough to successfully follow a more radical pathway than most.

They saw improvement in the vineyard as the top priority in order for the reds to achieve their potential. Consequently, they have worked on the use of minimal irrigation to increase yields, have introduced the Scott Henry trellis system to allow the grapes to ripen more effectively, have become more environmentally sensitive with the use of organically based fertilisers, the minimal use of herbicides and a more thoughtful pest management program.

There has been a dramatic improvement in the reds under Jürg Muggli and the Cabernets are now among the region's best. They are big, powerful wines with great richness, depth of flavour and quite firm, almost extractive tannins.

FORRESTAL FAVOURITES

1993 Secession
An attempt to break away from the name and style of the popular classic dry whites. It improves with short term bottle age when it becomes more restrained and elegant and has much softer acidity though still fresh, crisp and flavoursome with predominantly herbal and grassy characters.

Reserve Cabernets
Superbly crafted, these are rich, powerful wines of great complexity and impressive concentration showing plummy, dark cherry, raspberry and blackcurrant flavours and well-integrated charry oak. Although made for long term cellaring, they are supple and approachable now. The 1991 Reserve is quite vibrant and still has firm, fine grained tannins on the finish while the oak on the 1990 has softened and the 1989 is mouthfilling and generous yet with intense flavours.

Owners
Drs John Lagan and Eithne Sheridan

Chief Executive
Conor Lagan

Winemaker
Jürg Muggli

Established
1977

Production
190 tonnes
10,000 cases (1993)
12,000 cases (1994)

Area planted
16.5 ha.

Varieties planted

Chardonnay	3.5 ha.
Sauvignon Blanc	1.5 ha.
Semillon	5.0 ha.
Cabernet Franc	1.0 ha.
Cabernet Sauvignon	5.0 ha.
Merlot	0.5 ha.

Terry Road, Margaret River.
(Take Wallcliffe Road from the township, turn left at Railway Terrace, right into Terry Road and follow this gravel road for 2 km.)

Postal address
PO Box 144
MARGARET RIVER 6285

Phone (097) 572 581
Fax (097) 573 389

Hours of opening
10am to 5pm daily

Specialities
Bottles handpainted by artist-in-residence Robert Lawson: Xanadu Cabernet Franc $35, 1991 Xanadu Cabernet Sauvignon (magnums) $100.
Tee shirts, posters, corkscrews and glasses with Xanadu crest.

Wines produced

Xanadu Chardonnay	*$22.50*
Xanadu Secession A blend of semillon 65% and sauvignon blanc 35%.	*$14.50*
Xanadu Semillon (Reserve)	*$19.00*
Xanadu Featherwhite A dry Rosé style made from cabernet.	*$14.00*
Xanadu Cabernet Sauvignon (Reserve)	*$33.50*
Xanadu Cabernet Sauvignon	*$22.50*
Xanadu Noble Semillon	*$18.00*

YUNGARRA

IKE many of their colleagues, Gerry and Wendy Atherden are thriving after 'retiring' into the quiet life of Yungarra. Gerry was a business administrator with mining exploration companies including Western Mining and Alcoa. He has had the Dunsborough property for about twenty years and made the move from the city ten years ago. Wendy was a home economics teacher whose interest in the wine industry was aroused by working with Erl Happ and Brian Devitt at the nearby Busselton High School.

Gerry has taken responsibility for the vineyard and derives great satisfaction from having developed it, as much as possible, by himself. The vineyard is immaculately tendered and is highly regarded for the quality of its fruit. It was planted in stages from 1988 to 1990 with the first vintage in 1992.

The cellar door and restaurant were opened in January 1993 and these and the four chalets that have been established on the property are supervised by Wendy. Most of the Yungarra wine is sold from the cellar door which is close to the busy seaside resort of Dunsborough.

The wines are all made by Erl Happ: they have pristine fruit and are fresh and flavoursome. The Atherdens have chosen to produce easy drinking wines that are reasonably priced and they are keen to respond to customer preferences. For example, the Yungarra Estate Quartet (a blend of semillon, chenin, sauvignon blanc and verdelho) was dry in 1992 and a touch sweet in 1993. Although the Atherdens liked the 1992, the majority of their customers preferred the sweeter wine and so this is the style they will follow.

The best of their wines is the light bodied red, the first vintage of which won the silver medal in the 1993 Sheraton Awards, as runner up to the trophy winner in its category. The 1992 was a delightful, bargain-priced wine that was made to be drunk young. The red from 1993, a Cabernet Merlot, is a more substantial wine which has not been as popular with the Yungarra customers and so the 1994 red will be lighter-bodied in the style of the 1992.

FORRESTAL FAVOURITE

1992 Cabernet Sauvignon

Has perfumed, ripe plummy aromas, is soft yet full flavoured with good richness and concentration of flavour. It is a delicious, approachable, clean, well-made red, which has medium to light weight and gentle tannins.

Owners
Gerry and Wendy Atherden

Winemaker
Erl Happ

Established
1988

Production
60 tonnes
1200 cases (1993)
000 cases (1994)

Area planted
7.55 ha.

Varieties planted

Chenin Blanc	0.80 ha.
Sauvignon Blanc	1.60 ha.
Semillon	1.20 ha.
Verdelho	0.80 ha.
Cabernet Franc	0.40 ha.
Cabernet Sauvignon	1.00 ha.
Merlot	1.00 ha.
Pinot Noir	0.75 ha.

2 Yungarra Drive, Dunsborough.
(Turn off Caves Road, just east of
Dunsborough, into Commonage
Road and then right into Yungarra
Drive.
Or turn off Caves Road one km
west of Dunsborough directly into
Yungarra Drive.)

Postal address
PO Box 111
DUNSBOROUGH 6285

Phone: (097) 552 153
Fax: (097) 552 310

Hours of opening
10am to 4.30pm daily

Cafe
Morning & afternoon tea & lunch

Specialities
Chalets: $85 double/$49 single per
day bed and breakfast

Wines produced

Yungarra Estate Chenin Verdelho	*$11*
Yungarra Estate Quartet Semillon 65%, chenin 15%, sauvignon blanc 5% and verdelho5%: 1992 dry, 1993 touch of sweetness.	*$11*
Yungarra Estate Semillon Sauvignon	*$11*
Yungarra Estate Springtime A semi sweet blend of sauvignon blanc and verdelho.	*$10*
Yungarra Estate Pink Opal	*$10*
Yungarra Estate Cabernet Sauvignon	*$11*
Yungarra Estate Cabernet Port A light, fruity port made from cabernet sauvignon.	*$14*

The Margaret River Chardonnays

THERE is no question that, in a little more than two decades, Margaret River has carved a significant niche for itself within the Australian wine industry. Although responsible for little more than one per cent of the country's total grape production, Margaret River makes more than ten per cent of wines which sell at the premium end of the market. These do not merely rely on fiercely parochial locals for sales but are in demand both in the eastern states and overseas. In fact, the biggest problem facing local wineries is satisfying the demand for their treasures.

The Margaret River has two chardonnay superstars: Leeuwin Estate and Pierro, both of which are world class wines.

Leeuwin Estate Art Series Chardonnays

While it has been superbly promoted amidst the glitter of the famous Leeuwin Concerts and in the surroundings of one of the country's most attractive wineries, the Art Series Chardonnay has won Australian and international recognition for its sheer quality.

I was recently delighted to take part in a vertical tasting of five (1991, 1988, 1987, 1984 and 1981) of the Leeuwin Estate Art Series Chardonnays with winemaker, Bob Cartwright, and viticulturist, John Brocksopp. In this, as with the other vertical tasting of the wine that I've enjoyed, two things stand out. Firstly, the sheer quality of the wines and, secondly, their consistency.

The 1991 Leeuwin Estate Art Series Chardonnay is outstanding, perhaps as good as the 1986 or even the 1987. It has great depth of melon fruit and classy oak treatment.

The 1988 Leeuwin Estate Art Series Chardonnay is a bit closed although the palate shows luscious ripe peaches and melons and attractive barrel-ferment characters which are well-integrated with its powerful toasty oak. It is supple and round yet is tightly structured with a depth of rich, concentrated fruit and a long, oaky finish. This sophisticated wine will improve significantly with further aging as the wine opens out and reveals its opulence.

On a different occasion, chef, Jim McGuire, served lemon grilled chicken breast with tomato salsa on a bed of vegetable noodles with the 1988 Leeuwin Chardonnay. The spiciness of the dish was matched by the wine's complexity while the noodles provided textural variation and a bland backdrop which helped to highlight the chardonnay flavours.

The 1987 Leeuwin Estate Art Series Chardonnay is drinking beautifully with its lovely, characters of ripe melons and rich buttery oak, supple texture, great complexity and superb length. It has the balance, structure and depth of flavour to age gracefully over the next ten years.

I can't imagine the 1984 Leeuwin Estate Art Series Chardonnay getting much better than it is now, although it has the liveliness and persistence of flavour to live for many years. It has rich, developed chardonnay flavours, an almost unctuous mouth-feel, impressive complexity and great length.

After the tasting, I enjoyed drinking the wine at lunch with an excellent Margaret River marron salad with asparagus spears, melon balls, avocado and orange mayonnaise dressing in the restaurant at Leeuwin Estate. The intense citrus and toasty oak characters of the wine provided a delightful balance with the soft, rich flesh of the marron.

At a Wine and Food Society meeting, the 1984 Leeuwin Chardonnay was tasted alongside the 1984 Premier Cru Chablis 'Montmains' from the Domaine de la Maladière and served with a great Atlantic salmon dish. The Chablis was more pungent and less clean on the nose than the Leeuwin and by comparison lacked fruit in the mid-palate.

The point of the exercise was not to judge whether one wine was superior to the other, rather to look for points of comparison and difference between these two chardonnays the current releases of which retail for about the same price. Two factors need to be considered. Firstly, 1984 was not a very good year in Chablis and vintage variation is much more pronounced in France than in Margaret River. Secondly, most Australian wine lovers have cellar palates, that is they have a preference for styles which they are used to: such as, big, ripe, full-flavoured chardonnays. The exercise showed that Leeuwin Chardonnays retain their flavour and liveliness at a time when many Australian Chardonnays have become tired. They also look good when placed alongside similar wines from overseas.

The 1981 Leeuwin Estate Art Series Chardonnay was the wine that first focussed international attention on the winery and the Margaret River when it won the International Wine Challenge in London, a remarkable achievement with only its third crop. It is a delightful wine which is rich, supple and full-bodied, has ripe, herbaceous fruit and wonderful length with a slight tartness at the back from the young vines.

The question of price is never far away when talking about the Leeuwin Estate Chardonnay and it is usually a question of balancing undoubted quality with an expensive price tag. This is one of Western Australia's great wines, arguably its greatest. It's always on the short list of the wines that I want to show visitors from interstate or overseas.

There's a place in the market for Krug, Le Montrachet, Mouton Rothschild, Yquem and Grange. They represent the epitome of their styles and none of them come cheap. If you want to see just how good Western Australian chardonnay can get, then you need to taste the Leeuwin.

Keith Mugford of Moss Wood believes that Leeuwin Estate do not get enough credit for releasing their wines with bottle age. He says that to hold back the Moss Wood Chardonnay for a further three years would force its price up to about $40.

One of the ways in which Leeuwin have addressed the question of price has been to develop the cheaper Prelude range, the best of which have been the Chardonnay and the Cabernet, both very good, reasonably priced wines.

The 1991 Leeuwin Estate Prelude Chardonnay has powerful charry oak characters with peachy overtones, a supple, well-rounded with good weight on the mid-palate and a firm finish of reasonable length. This is a complex chardonnay that is good current drinking, especially with spicy chicken or robust seafood dishes.

There are substantial differences in cost between the Art Series and Prelude chardonnays. Both are one hundred per cent barrel fermented, the Art Series in new light grained French oak and the Prelude in one year old oak. The Art Series is aged on its lees in new oak for up to seventeen months while the Prelude is in barrel for a much shorter period, usually about nine months. After bottling, the Art Series is stored in temperature controlled conditions for two years longer than the Prelude.

As oak barrels currently cost Leeuwin $820 each and storage and handling costs are substantial, the treatment of the Arts Series chardonnay is expensive. Leeuwin Estate Managing Director, Dennis Horgan, estimates that the Art Series leaves the winery 150% more expensive than the Prelude because of the following additional costs:

Raw Materials and Barrels	30%
Racking, Storage and Handling	23%
Holding Costs at 12% interest	88%
Additional Profit	9%

Horgan has estimated that the additional profit which the winery makes from the $45 wine is less than $1 per bottle.

Leeuwin have clearly spared no expense in the pursuit of excellence. One can see that by touring the winery with its state-of-the-art equipment and storage facilities and by inspecting its meticulously tended vineyards.

The Pierro Chardonnays

As a vertical tasting conducted by Mike Peterkin showed, all of Pierro Chardonnays from 1986 to 1993 are outstanding wines and there is a remarkable consistency between them. They are all still fresh and lively with persistent flavours, impressive complexity and a seamless quality which indicates wonderful harmony between their fruit and oak.

The 1986, 1987 and 1988 wines may be close to their peak although I expect them to still be drinking beautifully in ten years time; it's not possible to say that about many Australian chardonnays. The 1986 shows some grassiness and honeyed aged characters while the 1988 has a voluminous bouquet with complex features including melon, toasty oak, yeast lees, nutty malolactic fermentation characters. Like those two wines, the 1987 Pierro Chardonnay is rich and concentrated with long, persistent flavours but it has greater intensity, complexity and power, appears mellow yet retains surprising fresh lemony, melony character and has an aftertaste that lingers seemingly forever. It's a great wine.

Another favourite of mine was the 1989 Pierro Chardonnay which is similarly multi-layered, has power, depth and length of flavour but even more intensity of ripe melons and delicate toasty oak on the nose.

The wines made between 1990 and 1993 all need plenty of time before they show their best. The 1990 Pierro Chardonnay has not yet opened up but has marvellous richness and concentration of flavour and great harmony while the 1991 which may be Pierro's best yet has ripe melon, peach and nutty, almondy characters, is mouthfilling and a great supple texture. The 1992 is tight, shows rich, spicy, buttery, melon and barrel ferment characters and has power with elegance and the 1993 is more delicate than the others but has fresh peach and melon characters complexed by toasty oak and hints of butterscotch.

The other Margaret River Chardonnays

If Leeuwin and Pierro are the undisputed stars of the region's chardonnays, then Moss Wood, Cullen, Evans and Tate and Cape Mentelle rank just a whisker behind them as each makes complex white wines of power, elegance and exquisite flavour.

The 1993 vintage was outstanding for white wines in Margaret River and the chardonnays are the best ever made at Evans and Tate and Cape Mentelle and second only to the 1990 at Moss Wood.

The 1992 Cullen Chardonnay is in line with the style developed by Vanya Cullen in recent years but shows more restraint. It has great intensity, richness and complex, nutty, leesy, barrel ferment characters in balance with its soft, ripe melony fruit.

While ripe citrus and melon fruit provides the substance of the 1993 Evans and Tate Margaret River Chardonnay, the wine's backbone comes from its complex oak handling which adds nuttiness and toasty barrel-ferment characters as well as the structure to enable it to age at least, in the medium term.

The 1993 Moss Wood Chardonnay is a substantial wine of great richness and concentration with toasty buttery oak, ripe grapefruit and melons and complexity from hints of butterscotch and caramel. As well as being soft and mouthfilling, it is powerful and long.

The vines from which the 1993 Cape Mentelle Chardonnay come are younger than the others in this bracket which may account for the slightly leaner style of the wine. This youthful, full flavoured white has ripe, peachy, melony fruit, well-integrated toasty oak and a zingy aftertaste.

The best of the next bracket are chardonnays from three of the region's newer enterprises - Devil's Lair, Voyager and Brookland Valley. All have made substantial investment, have carefully tendered vineyards and all employ Gary Baldwin of Oenotec as a consultant. Baldwin makes the Brookland Valley wines but there are excellent full-time winemakers at Devil's Lair and Voyager, in Janice McDonald and Stuart Pym respectively.

The 1993 Devil's Lair Chardonnay and the 1993 Brookland Valley Chardonnay are fruit driven styles. The former has more intense passionfruit, peach, smokey oak and barrel ferment characters while the latter has ripe peach, melon and toasty oak flavours. Both are fresh, clean, soft and delicious drinking. The 1993 Voyager Chardonnay has pristine cleanliness, some complexity, an attractive texture and rich and powerful melon and toasty oak flavours.

I had not previously tried tasting the same group of wines with two different tasting panels and thought it would be a fascinating exercise. In essence, there was a high degree of consensus among both groups about the best of the wines (that is, those already mentioned). However, with many of the other wines, there was more disagreement between the tasting panels and, between the individuals on each panel.

This mirrored the results of a three day wine assessment course run by the Australian Wine Research Institute in which I participated in late June. Thirty experienced tasters, including several show judges and many well-known winemakers achieved a greater degree of consensus on the best and worst wines than on those in the middle of the quality spectrum.

Of the wines not yet mentioned, I scored the Amberley, Happs and Leeuwin Estate Prelude as silver medal wines and the other wooded chardonnays as bronze medals. All are clean, well-made and flavoursome. Price and personal preference for a particular style of chardonnay will determine which of these you choose to buy.

The 1993 Amberley Chardonnay is a soft, easy drinking wine with delicate peach and tropical fruit although it is quite oaky; the 1993 Happs Chardonnay has powerful buttery oak and melon characters and a lively, crisp acidity; and the 1993

Leeuwin Estate Prelude has quite pungent melon and toasty oak aromas, mid-palate richness and high acidity on the finish.

The 1993 Moss Brothers Chardonnay and the 1993 Fermoy Chardonnay have quite strong oak characters with the latter having greater richness on the mid-palate and an appealing texture. Although the 1993 Lenton Brae Chardonnay lacks the intensity of the previous vintage it is soft and easy drinking.

Two other wines to have their supporters are the 1993 Ashbrook Chardonnay which is a well-made white with a touch of residual sugar while the 1993 Chateau Xanadu Chardonnay is rich and powerful with grapefruit, melon and toasty oak characters.

Without oak, I believe that Margaret River chardonnays lack varietal definition and intensity of flavour. This belief was reinforced when David Watson showed me an outstanding cask sample of his 1994 Woodlands Chardonnay from a new oak barrel which was worlds apart from his unwooded wine in the tasting.

The best of these unwooded wines was from a new label, the 1993 Vasse River Chardonnay which was soft, clean and fresh with grassy, figgy flavours and a touch of spiciness. while the 1993 Redgate Chardonnay showed similar grassy, passionfruit and yeasty characters but resembled a pleasant classic dry white rather than a chardonnay.

Recommended restaurants and cafes

THE restaurant and cafe scene has improved dramatically in the Margaret River region over the past year or two. There is a much greater choice of very good places at which to eat, especially at lunchtime, and the quality of the food being presented is better.

Another major improvement is that most restaurants provide appropriate wine glasses as part of the service they offer. Good wines deserve fine glassware.

Lack of consistency is a perennial problem in the hospitality industry and this is exacerbated in a region such as Margaret River, away from the metropolitan area, where the turnover of staff can be high. As far as service is concerned, the best places reduce this problem by implementing rigorous training programs. The loss of a chef can be more difficult to overcome. As much as is possible, I've been aware of the problem of consistency in producing the guide.

Every effort has been made to ensure that all details are accurate at the time of going to press. Where one price is quoted, it is the average for entrees, mains and desserts at each restaurant. Costly dishes, such as marron, prawns and lobster, are likely to be more expensive. Where no specific comments are made, the restaurant has no policy about smoking or there is no need for reservations unless you are part of a large party. Most restaurateurs prefer you to make a booking. Doing so gives you an opportunity to clarify or check on any details mentioned in this guide. At the time the book went to press, some of the newly opened cafes had not decided on what days they would open during winter, so it may pay to check with these.

Some of the licensed cafes may be prepared to allow you to bring a special bottle of premium wine in return for reasonable corkage, if you ring and ask.

Abbey Vale

(097) 552 277

Wildwood Road, Yallingup

The cellar door facility and restaurant, which sits on the edge of a purpose-built lake, is simple yet elegant. Whether you dine indoors or on the verandahs, you'll enjoy the tranquil ambience and the picturesque waterside views with a backdrop of tall gums trees and natural bush. Dishes may include an antipasto platter, a Kervella flan (goats cheese with Spanish onion), Cajun chicken salad, char-grilled venison fillet, South West beef fillet with creole prawns and hollandaise sauce and daily specials of soup, fish and pie.

Open daily
10.30 am-5pm.
Dishes
$7.50-$18.50.
Desserts
$5.

Abbey Vale wines served by the glass ($3.50) or bottle at cellar door prices and Moonshine ales by the bottle or jug; wheelchair access; smoking on verandahs and outside; smart casual dress; reservations recommended.

Arc of Iris

(097) 573 112

151 Bussell Highway, Margaret River

While the Arc still has an almost hippyish ambience thanks to the extremely dim lighting and the posters on the wall, there are now matching chairs at each table and uniform crockery and the cutlery. But if you want to drink good wine, you should bring your own glasses. Although the menu is a little static, Boon Loh's cooking is still very good and his food is fresh, flavoursome and inexpensive. Soups are very filling and there are many good vegetarian dishes such as fettuccine with walnuts, pumpkin and blue cheese, curry laksa and Thai salad with tofu. Lightly chargrilled ripe corn on the cob is succulent and not to be missed when available and the lamb and eggplant

Open
Wed-Sun 6 pm ➜
Entrees
$5.
Main Courses
$9-$10.
Desserts
$4.

is tender and spicy. The Duck, a char grilled confit served with an orange sauce, is the most expensive dish on the menu at $15 but no other dish is more than $10. While the service can be erratic, you should eat well and cheaply at this unique but eccentric cafe.

No credit cards. BYO; wheelchair access; casual dress; reservations recommended.

Amberley   (097) 552 288
Thorton Road, Yallingup

Picture book views set the scene for the invariably pleasant experience of a visit to Amberley. Casual outdoor eating takes place undercover amidst tranquil views: the vineyard and huge gum trees in the foreground, lush lawns flowing down to a thickly wooded watercourse with more vineyards and then gums lining the hillside opposite. The kitchen performs consistently and uses fresh produce to good effect. Dishes are always well presented and marry a range of textures and flavours in imaginative ways. The soups are highly recommended as are dishes such as charred eggplant sandwich; char-grilled seafood salad with oriental spices and chilli peanut sauce; Pemberton trout lightly grilled with a red pepper and chive semillon beurre blanc; grilled chicken breast with fresh herbs and walnuts with a hot ratatouille salad.

Open daily
10 to 4.30
Entrees
$4.50-$9.50.
Main Courses
$12.50-$13
Desserts
$5

The service is friendly and efficient. Wine is available by the glass or the bottle at cellar door prices.

Bay Cottage

(097) 553 554

Dunn Bay Road, Dunsborough

This purpose-built restaurant, situated between the turn-off from Caves Road and the Dunsborough Shopping Centre, was opened by Albert and Jillian Seth in 1986. It is capable of serving some of the best food in the region. There are two large rooms on either side of a large service desk which dominates the entrance. The atmosphere is quite formal with dim lighting, jarrah tables covered with white linen tablecloths and good quality tableware while the padded jarrah chairs are most comfortable. Interesting dishes include: smoked salmon and diced avocado with tortellini in a cream sauce with capers and dill; and tempura scallops with mango chilli coulis and shredded vegetable salad.

Open
Tues-Sat 7 pm→
Entrees
$9.50-$14.
Main Courses
$17.50-$20
Desserts
$7

BYO, no corkage; wheelchair access to restaurant but not to toilets; smart casual; reservations recommended.

The Berry Farm

(097) 575 054

Bessell Road, Margaret River

This small cafe serves uncomplicated but good country food at very reasonable prices. Items on the menu include soup and gourmet pie of the day; picker's platter (ham, salami, pate, cheese, olives); scones, muffins, cakes, coffee and tea. Wines are available by the glass or bottle at cellar door prices.

Open daily
10 am to 4 pm.
Entrees
$5
Main Courses
$6.50-$12
Desserts
$2.50-$4.50

ALL CREDIT CARDS

BYO, no corkage; wheelchair access; smoking on verandahs and outside; casual dress.

Cafe Forte   (097) 573 101
101 Bussell Highway, Margaret River

This cafe has been producing interesting, good quality food. Light snacks such as soup, bruschetta, nachos, sandwiches and quiche of the day cater for lunch time diners while there is a particularly strong vegetarian selection including tofu burgers, interesting and complex spinach, Greek and Thai salads, ceviche (marinated fish) and malfiati (spinach and ricotta gnocchi with tomato sauce). The menu also includes pastas, sirloin steak and several daily dinner specials. Good coffee and a reasonable range of teas.

BYO, corkage $1.50; wheelchair access; casual dress.

Open
Thurs-Mon
11 am until late.
Entrees
$5-$9.50.
Main Courses
$10.50-$13
Desserts
$4.50-$5

bankcard   MasterCard   VISA

Cafe Ibis   (097) 553 381
Dunsborough Village, Dunsborough

Robert Goble, former chef at the Jolly Frog in Perth, is serving some of the most imaginative and flavoursome food in the region at remarkably cheap prices. He and his wife, Michelle who manages front-of-house, have converted a small shop near the newsagency. While the venue has limitations, especially because of its size, the polished pine tables and chairs are comfortable and the place has a relaxed ambience. Entrees may include a spicy, piquant pumpkin soup with chives and sour cream, wok fried beef and vegetables with satay sauce or wild mussels in a sweet chilli sauce. Mains could include tender and rare Moroccan grilled lamb fillet on couscous with yoghurt and coriander or braised rabbit in red wine and fresh, herb provencal with grilled polenta. The

Open for dinner
Daily in summer
Tues-Sat in winter
Entrees
$4.50-$7.50.
Main Courses
$12.50-$15
Desserts
$4.50

desserts are show stoppers and include very filling, sticky date pudding and chocolate and peanut fudge cakes. The service is attentive and thoughtful.

BYO, corkage 50c; wheelchair access reasonable; casual dress; reservations necessary on weekends and in summer.

Cafe Contadino   (097) 553 960
Seymour House, Dunn Bay Road, Dunsborough

This large, lively cafe, which features an open kitchen and a large outdoor area shaded by umbrellas, specialises in Italian country cooking. It showed enough potential, when visited in its first week of operation, to suggest that it will be around for quite some time. Although there were teething problems with the menu and some of the rustic furniture was decidedly uncomfortable, part owner/chef, Nino Zoccali, is passionate about his food and some of the dishes were excellent. The prawns were perfectly cooked, the veal delightfully tender, the coffee was good and the lemon tart, light and flavoursome. The menu offers many traditional peasant dishes and includes five pasta sauces with a choice of fettuccine, gnocchi, linguini, penne and spaghetti.

Open daily
10 am-late in summer.
Check winter hours.
Entrees
$4.50-$9.50.
Main Courses
$12.50-$17.90
Desserts
$3.90

Wheelchair access; casual dress; reservations recommended.

Cullen   (097) 555 277
Caves Road, Willyabrup

The cafe at Cullen is an ideal place to eat if you have planned a busy day touring wineries and would prefer not to linger over lunch. The food is fresh, light and full of flavour and features local produce. Dishes include: delicious soups; open continental sandwiches; Greek salad with local fetta; port and fig pate; Margaret River cheeseboard; vineyard selection (meats, pates, cheese) and cakes to tempt you over a cup of excellent coffee or one of their many teas. Eat outdoors or at the long wooden tables and benches in the barrel hall.

Open daily
10am to 4pm.
Dishes
$7-$10
Desserts
$2.50

No credit cards. Cullen wines served at cellar door prices, no BYO; wheelchair access; casual dress.

The Flame Tree Restaurant   (097) 555 422
Bussell Highway, Cowaramup

One wonders how the onslaught of triplets will affect this fine restaurant. I expect chef/owner, Hamish McLeay will survive the experience but it will certainly be a few months before his wife, Jane, returns to her rightful position at front of house. However, the staff is so well trained and efficient that I expect the restaurant to function well even without Jane at the helm. Hamish is an outstanding chef who continues to cook with confidence, showing flair and imagination with dishes such as grilled tiger prawns served with wilted autumn greens flavoured with ginger juice and peanut oil; local scallops served with homemade spaghetti tomato and sesame juice; local venison rolled around a vegetable and sweet mustard stuffing, baked and served with a meat glaze. His gravlax is

Open for dinner
Fri-Wed.
Entrees
$9
Main Courses
$18
Desserts
$6

simplicity itself but sensational and the homemade ravioli filled with venison liver pate served with a chive and mustard cream sauce is more complex and likewise memorable. Almost all dishes are available as an entree or a main course. Certainly one of the best restaurants in the region.

BYO. Wheelchair access reasonable; casual dress; bookings essential.

Flutes Cafe (097) 556 250
Brookland Valley Vineyard, Caves Road, Willyabrup

Overlooking a dam on the Willyabrup Brook with tall gums and vineyards framing the backdrop, Flutes can boast the most picturesque setting in the region. There are three dining areas: indoors, outdoors and outdoors under cover and the place has a casual yet stylish cafe atmosphere. A tasting of Brookland Valley wines is available at the table. The menu is most comprehensive and changes with the seasons. It may include an

Open
Tues-Sun
11 am to 4.30 pm for lunch, coffee and cakes.
Dinner
Sat from 7pm
Entrees
$6-$12.50
Main Courses
$16.50-$19.50
Desserts
$8

ALL CREDIT CARDS

eggplant and goat's cheese sandwich with pesto, oak smoked venison rump and the most stunning yet simple dish I've tried there: fresh marron sandwiched in a sesame-buttermilk burger bun with herb mayo. The cheese platters and decadent desserts are worth lingering over. Coffee is well-made and a wide range of Indian and herbal teas are available. Service, under the direction of Dee Jones, is very good.

Brookland Valley wines available by the glass or bottle, no BYO; wheelchair access; smart casual dress; bookings necessary.

Leeuwin Estate Restaurant   (097) 576 253
Stevens Road, Margaret River

The drawcard of this beautiful restaurant is its idyllic setting overlooking the gardens of Leeuwin Estate with its wonderful backdrop of tall gums, site of the famous Leeuwin Concerts. Seating is quite informal on long jarrah tables and benches in the dining room or on jarrah garden furniture on the verandah or balcony. The food is at its best when closest to country cooking: roasted sweet pepper and black olive soup; roasted lamb shank with rosemary and garlic; winter pie of chicken and leek with a light meat glaze. Service is outstanding: knowledgeable, efficient and friendly.

Open
12 to 2.30 daily
Sat dinner 7pm→
Entrees
$5-$9
Main Courses
$14-$17 (plus side dishes)
Desserts
$6

ALL CREDIT CARDS

Leeuwin Estate wines only, no BYO; wheelchair access; non-smoking area; smart casual dress; reservations necessary.

Newtown House   (097) 554 485
Bussell Highway, Vasse

The region's best chef, Stephen Reagan, and his wife Barbara own this small, comfortable two room restaurant in a restored settlers stone cottage built in 1851. Reagan's food is consistent and excellent: outstanding produce presented as flavoursome and complex dishes which provide a range of interesting tastes and textures. These may include: salad of king prawns with ginger, coriander and buckwheat noodles; linguine with trout in a cream and white wine sauce; breast of duck with a pinot jelly and duck confit cassoulet; medallions of pork with muscat and grapes. Excellent unobtrusive

Open
10 am-5 pm daily for afternoon teas and lunch.
Dinner Wed-Sat.
Entrees
$8.50-$13.50
Main Courses
$16.50-$19.50
Desserts
$6.50

service. There is still good choice from the more limited lunch menu and it's cheaper.

Wheelchair access; no smoking; smart casual dress; reservations necessary for dinner.

Rivendell Bistro   (097) 552 090
Wildwood Road, Yallingup

Even JRR Tolkein would have been well pleased with the view, looking across beautifully kept gardens and lawns that roll down to a tree lined watercourse while the hillside opposite is covered with large native gums. There's a warm fire in winter and comfortable furniture inside and outdoors.

The food at Rivendell is good quality, home-made country fare. A winter lunch is likely to include a selection of three soups (such as country pumpkin, beef mulligatawny and chunky mushroom) and specials such as Neapolitan frittata with salad or hot beef roll in red wine and onion gravy. Items on the standard menu are also available picnic style to take onto the terrace or lawns. These include a garden fresh salad, country platter, cheese board or bread and pickles. Snacks such as scones, biscuits, cakes, fruit pie, icecreams and cheese plate are available.

Open daily
10 am-5 pm for snacks or Devonshire tea.
Lunches 11 to 3
Dishes
$5-$8.50
Desserts
$4.50

Rivendell wines or BYO; wheelchair access; smoking preferred on covered verandah or terrace; casual dress.

Rivers Bar and Brasserie   (097) 572 655

Margaret River Hotel, Bussell Hwy, Margaret River

This hotel is a major hub of the Margaret River township where marketing consultants, property developers or wine makers meet to discuss business or join the tourists in lazing away the hours eating the brasserie food and drinking the local wines or some of the eleven draught beers on tap. The regularly changing menu may include a curry, a pasta dish, market fresh fish and treats like Cajun salad and chilli mussels. While the service is efficient, the quality of the food has lacked consistency.

Fully licensed; wheelchair access; non-smoking area for diners; reservations preferred.

Open daily
8 to 10 am for breakfast
12 to 2.30 lunch
6 to 8.30 dinner.
Entrees
$8
Main courses
$17.50
Desserts
$4

ALL CREDIT CARDS

Spaghetti Bowl   (097) 572 999

Bussell Highway, Margaret River

The restaurant occupies a single, large, split-level, octagonal-shaped room with high pine ceiling, red carpet and rammed earth walls. The menu is predictable and typical of a middle-of-the-road Italian restaurant. Many dishes have reasonable flavour but lack finesse in presentation. If you are looking for a quick, undemanding, reasonably priced meal, you are unlikely to be disappointed. The service is friendly and helpful.

Licensed and BYO, $2 corkage; wheelchair access from back; smoking in bar area only; casual dress; bookings essential on weekends.

Open
Tues-Sun 6 pm→
Entrees
$7
Main Courses
$14
Desserts
$4

bankcard MasterCard VISA

La Trattoria

(097) 553 040

Caves Road, Dunsborough

Situated two kilometres east of Dunsborough at the Bananmah Wildlife Park, this cafe occupies a large high ceiling room with a smaller room to the side. The main area is quite dark during the daytime in spite of having almost floor to ceiling windows on three sides. Pleasant views of the bushland setting of the Wildlife Park partly compensate for this. Its casual atmosphere is enhanced by being furnished with pine chairs and tables. The food is reasonably priced and is of an acceptable standard. Interesting dishes include: panfried calamari with pistachios, dried tomato, garlic and chilli; potato and herb gnocchi; oven roasted chicken with pesto cream, black olives and spaghetti; veal scaloppine with a lemon and pesto sauce on a vegetable risotto. Woodfired pizzas are available, except on Saturday, and include a calzone (folded pizza) and a sfinciuni (a thin pizza sandwich). The coffee is disappointing. Seats 100 inside and 30 outside.

Open daily
10 am until late
Entrees
$5-$12
Main Courses
$11-$19
Desserts
$5

Licensed and BYO, $3 corkage; wheelchair access; no smoking; casual dress; bookings recommended at night.

Vasse Felix   (097) 555 242
Caves Road, Willyabrup

This outstanding brasserie occupies the first floor of a large rustic, stone building which overlooks the vineyard. It features huge wooded beams, large windows, a warm central fire in winter and an undercover outdoor area with wooden garden furniture. Inside, there are classy, wooden edged tables with comfortable upholstered cane chairs. The food is imaginative, well presented, flavoursome and reasonably priced: dhufish wing and roasted tomato soup with prawn and dhufish wontons; yabbie and asparagus salad; green masala lamb curry; herb crusted veal cutlet with apple and aubergine ratatouille and ginger and banana sticky pudding with coconut icecream. Professional service. Good coffee.

Open daily
10am until late
Entrees
$5-$8.50
Main Courses
$15-$18.50
Desserts
$6

ALL CREDIT CARDS

Vasse Felix wines are available by the glass or bottle at slightly above cellar door prices. Most who dine at Vasse Felix prefer to enjoy a reasonably paced, leisurely lunch. If you want a quicker meal, ask when you arrive.

Vineyard Cafe   (097) 553 331
Meelup Beach Road, Meelup

Set atop the limestone winery on the side of a hill, this purpose-built cafe overlooks vineyards and densely treed bushlands and has sweeping views of the nearby ocean. The entrance to the cafe, which is paved with terracotta tiles, is dominated by the tasting bar from which samples of Wise wines are offered. There are two dining areas, the more elegant, carpeted indoor area which has rendered limestone walls on two side and floor to ceiling windows on the other sides while the sheltered wooden verandah has the same iron-framed, cane-covered chairs with pine tables. The food shows flair, is well presented and the menu, which changes daily, is well-balanced and caters for all tastes. The dishes are thoughtfully constructed and have abundant flavour and interesting textual variation. The soups are recommended as are dishes such as crumbed Fremantle sardine fillets served on a Greek salad with aioli; pork fillets braised with baby onions, potatoes, red peppers and brussel sprouts in a cabernet jus; and French lamb cutlets char-grilled served with ratatouille and a basil jus. Service is extremely professional: thoughtful, efficient and unobtrusive.

Open for lunch
Wed-Sun 11am-4pm.
Dinner
Fri-Sat 6pm
Thurs in summer
Long weekends
Lunch Mon
Dinner Sun
Entrees
$8.75-11.50
Main Courses
$15.50-$18.50
Desserts
$6.50

Wise wines at cellar door prices or BYO with $5 corkage; wheelchair access; no smoking in cafe; dress, smart casual; reservations recommended for weekends.

Wildwood   (097) 552 066
Caves Road, Yallingup

The high prices and the notice on the menu that good food takes time signal that this is a restaurant rather than a brasserie. Still it is an impressive looking place and the food is good. There is undercover dining outside. The lunch menu is available all day and is simpler and slightly less expensive than for dinner. The dishes are quite complex and match a range of flavours and textures in generally successful combinations. These include pan fried veal with red wine glaze and herb linguine; Moroccan chicken breast; local dhufish panfried with lemon sauce; and oven-baked rack of lamb with an apricot and mint jus served with lemon and pinenut rice. The desserts are superb. Service is quite casual but attentive and helpful. One pleasing touch is that iced water is placed on the table immediately after arrival. The wine glasses are thick and heavy though of a reasonable shape.

Open daily
9.30 am till late.
Entrees
$12-$15
Main Courses
$23-$28
Desserts
$7.50

BYO (no corkage) or wines by the glass for $4 or at slightly above cellar door prices; wheelchair access; non-smoking restaurant, smoking only at bar or outside; smart casual dress; reservations recommended.

Yungarra   (097) 552 153
Yungarra Drive, Dunsborough

Panoramic views of the countryside and the ocean are a highlight of any visit to Yungarra but there is also an opportunity to taste the wines or to relax either indoors or outside. Wendy Atherden is a former Home Economics teacher who serves tasty home cooking at very reasonable (actually cheap) prices: a generous meal can be had for $12.

Open
Fri-Wed
10 am-4.30 pm
Summer: 9 am-5 pm
Entrees
$5
Main Courses
$12
Desserts
$4

Lunches include soup of the day; baked stuffed jacket potato; quiche and salad; local smoked fish; the Yungarra starter platter (local cheeses, smoked local fish, venison sausage with home-made bread); and a vigneron's lunch (Virginia ham, cheese and dill pickle with salad and home-made bread). Regular desserts are cheesecake, apple crumble and ice cream.

Yungarra wines or BYO; wheelchair access; no smoking inside; reservations recommended.

Other restaurants and cafes

1885 Restaurant   (097) 573 177
Farrelly Street, Margaret River

Open Tuesday to Saturday from 7pm.
Entrees $9, mains $22, desserts $7.50.
All credit cards; licensed; wheelchair access but not to toilets;
no smoking except in lounge; smart casual dress; reservations
recommended.

Basil Bush Restaurant   (097) 573 735
Colonial Motel, Wallcliffe Road, Margaret River

Open daily from 6 to 8.30pm.
Entrees $8.50. mains $14 plus vegetables, green salad or chips
$2.50, desserts $6;
BYO no corkage; wheelchair access but not to toilets; non-
   smoking; smart casual dress; reservations
recommended.

Bootleg Brewery   (097) 556 300
Pusey Road, Willyabrup

Open daily from 10am to 4.30pm.
Light snacks, sandwiches, salads, cheeseboard, antipasto,
beefsteak pie, all under $10 and ploughman's lunch $12.50.
   Good wheelchair access; casual dress; reservations
recommended.

Casuarina Restaurant   (097) 572 033
Captain Freycinet Inn, Bussell Highway, Margaret River

Open daily from 7am until 8pm.
Entrees $11, mains $17, desserts $7.
All credit cards; licensed; no wheelchair access; no smoking
restaurant; smart casual dress; reservations recommended.

Caves House   (097) 552 131
Yallingup

Open daily from 6am until 9pm.

Entrees $10, mains $15, desserts $6.50.
Licensed and BYO, $5 corkage; wheelchair access poor;
no smoking; smart casual dress.

Crayfish Inn   (097) 552 101
Cnr Canal Rocks & Caves Road, Yallingup

Open Thurs-Mon. for dinner, Sat-Sun for lunch.

Entrees $8.50, mains $17.50, desserts $5.50.
Licensed or BYO wines only, $2 corkage; wheelchair
access difficult; separate smoking area.

Harry's Mexican Wave   (097) 572 703
Bussell Highway, Margaret River

Open Wednesday to Sunday from 6pm.

Entrees $6, mains $8.50, desserts $3.50.
BYO, 50c corkage; casual dress.

Larian's Restaurant   (097) 576 448
Lot 36 Bussell Highway, Witchcliffe.
Open Tuesday to Saturday from 6.30pm.

Entrees $7.50; mains $18.50; desserts $5.90.
BYO, corkage $2 per bottle. wheelchair access but
difficult to toilet; no smoking except in smoker's lounge.

Margaret River Chinese   (097) 572 788
133 Bussell Highway, Margaret River

Open from 5.30pm daily in summer holidays (late December
to early February). Wednesdays to Sundays at other times.

Lunch Thurs and Fri from 12 to 2pm.
BYO, corkage $2 per bottle.

Marron Farm Cafe
(097) 576 279

Wickham Road, Margaret River

From September to April, open daily 10am to 4pm. From May to July, open Tuesday to Sunday 11am till 4pm. Closed August.

 Corkage $2 per bottle; wheelchair access but not to toilets; no smoking; casual dress.

Nookery Cafe
(097) 557 547

Woody Nook, Metricup Road, Willyabrup

Open daily from 11am until 3pm.

 Entrees $5, mains $11, desserts $3.50.
No corkage; wheelchair access; no smoking.

The Rocks Restaurant
(097) 552 332

Smiths Beach Road, Yallingup

Open Tue-Sat for dinner.
Entrees $9, mains $16.

 Licensed or BYO, corkage $2 per table; wheelchair access but not to toilets; casual dress.

Swell Cafe and Restaurant
(097) 555 030

Gracetown

Restaurant open from 6pm Tuesday to Sunday.
Entrees $7.50, mains $14, desserts $4.50.

 Licensed; wheelchair access but not to toilets; casual dress.

Surfside
(097) 552 133

Yallingup Beach

Open on weekdays from 11am - 3pm and from 6pm until close: on weekends from 10 am until late.

 Licenced and BYO, corkage $3 per bottle; wheelchair access; casual dress; bookings recommended.

What's open for lunch

FRIDAY
- Abbey Vale
- Amberley
- Bootleg Brewery
- Berry Farm
- Cafe Swell
- Cafe Forte
- Caffe Contadino
- C Gnarburup(s)
- Casuarina
- Caves House
- Cullen
- Flutes
- Leeuwin
- MR Chinese
- Marron Farm
- Newtown H
- Rivendell
- Rivers
- Sea Gardens
- Surfside
- La Trattoria
- Vasse Felix
- Vineyard C
- Wildwood
- Woody Nook
- Yungarra

SATURDAY
- Abbey Vale
- Amberley
- Bootleg Brewery
- Berry Farm
- Cafe Swell
- Cafe Forte
- Caffe Contadino
- C Gnarburup (s)
- Casuarina
- Caves House
- Crayfish Inn
- Cullen
- Flutes
- Leeuwin
- Marron Farm
- Newtown H
- Rivendell
- Rivers
- Sea Gardens
- Surfside
- La Trattoria
- Vasse Felix
- Vineyard C
- Wildwood
- Woody Nook
- Yungarra

SUNDAY
- Abbey Vale
- Amberley
- Bootleg Brewery
- Berry Farm
- Cafe Swell
- Cafe Forte
- Caffe Contadino
- C Gnarburup (s)
- Casuarina
- Caves House
- Crayfish Inn
- Cullen
- Flutes
- Leeuwin
- Marron Farm
- Newtown H
- Rivendell
- Rivers
- Sea Gardens
- Surfside
- La Trattoria
- Vasse Felix
- Vineyard C
- Wildwood
- Woody Nook
- Yungarra

MONDAY
- Abbey Vale
- Amberley
- Bootleg Brewery
- Berry Farm
- Cafe Forte
- Caffe Contadino
- C Gnarburup (s)
- Casuarina
- Caves House
- Cullen
- Leeuwin
- Marron F (s)
- Newtown H
- Rivendell
- Rivers
- Sea Gardens
- Surfside
- La Trattoria
- Vasse Felix
- Wildwood
- Woody Nook
- Yungarra

TUESDAY
- Abbey Vale
- Amberley
- Bootleg Brewery
- Berry Farm
- Cafe Swell
- Caffe Contadino
- C Gnarburup (s)
- Casuarina
- Caves House
- Cullen
- Flutes
- Leeuwin
- Marron Farm
- Newtown H
- Rivendell
- Rivers
- Sea Gardens
- Surfside
- La Trattoria
- Vasse Felix
- Wildwood
- Woody Nook
- Yungarra

WEDNESDAY
- Abbey Vale
- Amberley
- Bootleg Brewery
- Berry Farm
- Cafe Swell
- Caffe Contadino
- C Gnarburup(s)
- Casuarina
- Caves House
- Cullen
- Flutes
- Leeuwin
- Marron Farm
- Newtown H
- Rivendell
- Rivers
- Sea Gardens
- Surfside
- La Trattoria
- Vasse Felix
- Vineyard C
- Wildwood
- Woody Nook
- Yungarra

THURSDAY
- Abbey Vale
- Amberley
- Bootleg Brewery*
- Berry Farm
- Cafe Swell*
- Cafe Forte
- Caffe Contadino*
- C Gnarburup (s)
- Casuarina
- Caves House
- Cullen
- Flutes
- Leeuwin
- MR Chinese
- Marron Farm
- Newtown H
- Rivendell
- Rivers
- Sea Gardens
- Surfside
- La Trattoria
- Vasse Felix
- Vineyard C
- Wildwood
- Woody Nook

(s) *summer only*   * *check for winter hours*

What's open for dinner

FRIDAY
- Arc of Iris
- Basil Bush
- Bay Cottage
- Cafe Forte
- Cafe Ibis
- Caffe Contadino
- Casuarina
- Caves House
- Crayfish Inn
- 1885
- Flame Tree
- Harry's Mexican
- Larian's
- Mama's Oriental
- MR Chinese
- Newtown House
- Rivers MR Hotel
- The Rocks
- Spaghetti Bowl
- Swell Restaurant
- Surfside
- La Trattoria
- Vineyard Cafe
- Wildwood

SATURDAY
- Arc of Iris
- Basil Bush
- Bay Cottage
- Cafe Forte
- Cafe Ibis
- Caffe Contadino
- Casuarina
- Caves House
- Crayfish Inn
- 1885
- Flame Tree
- Flutes
- Harry's Mexican
- Larian's
- Leeuwin Estate
- Mama's Oriental
- MR Chinese
- Newtown House
- Rivers MR Hotel
- The Rocks
- Spaghetti Bowl
- Swell Restaurant
- Surfside
- La Trattoria
- Vineyard Cafe
- Wildwood

SUNDAY
- Arc of Iris
- Basil Bush
- Cafe Forte
- Cafe Ibis (s)
- Caffe Contadino
- Casuarina
- Caves House
- Crayfish Inn
- Flame Tree
- Harry's Mexican
- Mama's Oriental
- MR Chinese
- Rivers MR Hotel
- Spaghetti Bowl
- Swell Restaurant
- Surfside
- La Trattoria
- Wildwood

MONDAY
- Basil Bush
- Cafe Forte
- Cafe Ibis (s)
- Caffe Contadino
- Casuarina
- Caves House
- Crayfish Inn
- Flame Tree
- MR Chinese (s)
- Rivers MR Hotel
- Surfside
- La Trattoria
- Wildwood

TUESDAY
- Basil Bush
- Bay Cottage
- Cafe Ibis
- Caffe Contadino
- Casuarina
- Caves House
- 1885
- Flame Tree
- Larian's
- MR Chinese (s)
- Rivers MR Hotel
- The Rocks
- Spaghetti Bowl
- Swell Restaurant
- Surfside
- La Trattoria
- Wildwood

WEDNESDAY
- Arc of Iris
- Basil Bush
- Bay Cottage
- Cafe Ibis
- Caffe Contadino
- Casuarina
- Caves House
- 1885
- Flame Tree
- Harry's Mexican
- Larian's
- Mama's Oriental
- MR Chinese
- Newtown House
- Rivers MR Hotel
- The Rocks
- Spaghetti Bowl
- Swell Restaurant
- Surfside
- La Trattoria
- Wildwood

THURSDAY
- Arc of Iris
- Basil Bush
- Bay Cottage
- Cafe Forte
- Cafe Ibis
- Caffe Contadino
- Casuarina
- Caves House
- Crayfish Inn
- 1885
- Harry's Mexican
- Larian's
- Mama's Oriental
- MR Chinese
- Newtown House
- Rivers MR Hotel
- The Rocks
- Spaghetti Bowl
- Swell Restaurant *
- Surfside
- La Trattoria
- Vineyard Cafe (s)
- Wildwood

(s) summer only   * check for winter hours

Fast food in Margaret River

F AST food in Margaret River is pretty much the same as you'll find anywhere else. The fast food places define themselves by serving pre-prepared meals which are heated in bain maries or microwaves or by serving food such as hamburgers, fish and chips or pizzas which can be cooked quickly. There will be times when most of us will want to or need to take advantage of the convenience and cheapness that they offer but their quality will rarely match that of a good cafe or restaurant where meals are prepared individually on request.

The problem with giving details of fast food outlets is that they tend to change hands regularly, rendering a guide such as this out of date. These fast food outlets are recommended.

Cafe Gnarbrup   (097) 572 747
Prevelly Park

This open air cafe is perfectly located on the beach at Prevelly, and is under the same ownership as the Sea Gardens Cafe. It is only open from December to June. The dinner menu may include dishes such as: dhufish chowder; eggplant flan; fennel and olive frittata; Thai lamb and pork parcels; fresh Augusta dhufish. The lunch menu is more limited and may include dishes such as: soup of the day; nachos; salads; fish of the day; tempeh, beef and fish burgers. In my experience, the coffee has been disappointing.

Open from 7am until late for breakfast, lunch and dinner and for drinks and cakes.

Mama's Oriental Takeaway   (097) 572 622
Bussell Highway, Margaret River

This small but busy cafe serves outstanding fast food to customers who dine in or take away. The blackboard menu includes Chinese, Indonesian and Indian dishes such as chicken spring rolls, dahl, potato, chicken or beef curry, sweet and sour fish, chilli squid, fried rice and noodles. Diners can choose from the menu or combination platters (meat, rice and 2 vegetables for $8; 2 meat, 2 vegetables and rice for $9; everything for $10). Clearly the best fast food in the region.

Open Wednesday to Sunday from 5.30 to 9pm. Closed during August. No bookings. No credit cards.

Margaret River Wholefood Bakehouse   (097) 572 194
31 Station Road, Margaret River

Situated at the top of the town, off Wallcliffe Road, this small takeaway lunch bar serves wholesome breads, pizzas, spanokopita, a wide range of pies (such as curried lentil, cauliflower and broccoli, chicken and vegetable). Many healthy cakes and slices and milkshakes are also available.

Sea Gardens Cafe   (097) 573 074
Prevelly Park

The ocean views are superb and, although the furnishing is basic, this popular cafe serves good quality fast food at cheap prices all year round. Burgers, pizzas, sandwiches, foccacia and stir fry are available to dine in or take away. Fresh fish either deep fried or grilled is a speciality.

Open daily from 8.30am until 10.30pm.

Swell Cafe   (097) 555 030
Gracetown

This cafe in the day / restaurant at night, formerly the Gallery and Bayview Cafe, has indoor and outdoor dining areas with stunning views of the bay at Gracetown. It serves reasonable quality fast food such as lentil, tempeh, chicken and hamburgers, Lebanese rolls and sandwiches.

Open Tues - Sun 9am to 6pm.

Produce of the Region

THE following is a selection of the Margaret River region's best food attractions plus the Bootleg Brewery. Most are not open on Christmas Day, Boxing Day, New Year's Day and Good Friday.

The Berry Farm   (097) 575 054
Bessell Road, Margaret River

Pick your own fruit in season: fresh produce such as strawberries, raspberries, boysenberries, kiwi and nashi fruit is available except during the winter months. The Berry Farm produces a range of eleven fruit wines including ones made from kiwi fruit, plum, pear, boysenberry as well as raspberry wine, strawberry, pear, cider, herb, honey, red and white wine vinegars. In addition, they market more than twenty jams or conserves and preserves such as brandy cumquats, preserved figs, prunes in plum port and shiraz jelly. All are available for tasting.

Open daily from 10am until 4.30pm.

Bootleg Brewery   (097) 556 300
Pusey Road, Willyabrup

Situated on Wildberry Road near the corner of Johnson and Pusey Roads, the brewery is housed in a striking, large, mudbrick building with a wooden upstairs gallery and tower overlooking a dam. Although the surrounds are as yet unfinished, the venue is already popular and, in time, should look superb. All the Bootleg beers are available for tasting. At the time of going to press, these were two bitter ales. There are plans to produce a stout, pilsener or a lighter coloured ale and a low alcohol pale ale. The beers are available by the glass and jug and the wines of two local wineries, (such as Ribbon Vale, Moss Brothers and Clairault) chosen on a rotation basis, are for sale with a meal. Light lunches and cheap snacks such as the following are served: sandwiches, salads, cheeseboard, antipasto, ploughman's lunch, beefsteak pie. Good wheelchair access; casual dress; reservations recommended.

Open daily from 10am to 4.30pm.

Fonti's Dairy Factory　　　　(097) 557 588
Bussell Highway, Cowaramup

Situated 15 kilometres north of Margaret River just past the junction with Harmans Mill Road, Fonti's produce a range of specialty cheeses, yoghurts and cream which are available for tasting and for purchase. There is also a window to view cheese making and a display of historical dairy artifacts.

Open 10 am - 3pm daily.

Margaret River Cheese Company　(097) 555 400
Bussell Highway, Cowaramup

Situated about a kilometre south of Fonti's and now owned by them, the Margaret River Cheese Company still produces a fine range of cheeses including their signature brie as well as a camembert, some cheddars and fettas. These are available for tasting and purchase.

Open Monday to Friday 9am - 3pm, weekends 11am - 4pm.

Marron Farm Cafe   (097) 576 279
Wickham Road, Margaret River

The region's only commercial marron farm is situated 11km south of Margaret River. It has playground, swimming pool and barbecue facilities that are open to the public as well as a cafe which specialises in marron lunches. Inspections of the marron farm can be arranged during opening hours.

Open daily 10am to 4pm from September to April.

From May to July, open Tuesday to Sunday from 11am till 4pm. Closed August.

Rivendell Gardens   (097) 552 090
Wildwood Road, Yallingup

Set amidst beautiful herb and cottage gardens, flowing lawns and natural bushland, Rivendell has something for everyone: from delicious homely snacks or lunches to tastings of wine or the huge range of top quality jams, chutneys and sauces produced under the Rivendell label. The upstairs gallery is likely to be exhibiting the work of some local artist and the grounds make an ideal spot for the perfect picnic. You can pick your own strawberries in season.

Open daily, 10am - 5pm.

Art and Craft Galleries

Cowaramup Pottery   (097) 555 467
Bussell Highway, Cowaramup

A visit to several contemporary potteries while holidaying in England led Gary Nichol to a fine arts course in which he majored in ceramics at the Warrnambool Institute. Four footloose years saw Gary buffalo hunting and building houses in the Northern Territory and crayfishing off the Western Australian coast, before heading for the surf of Margaret River. Impressed by the potential of the region, Gary purchased the old butcher's shop in Cowaramup and transformed it into a working studio complete with wood fired kiln in 1981.

Since then Gary and Sonja Nicol have developed a reputation for producing functional pottery with bold glazes: such as striking pink and snow white. Among the most popular are floral patterns and schooling fish in pink or the green leaf pattern with salmon coral gumnuts on a snow white background. The stoneware includes coffee cups, dip trays, vases, tea pots, cutlery drains, demi johns, serving platters, salad bowls and pie dishes. Many items such as dinner sets and vinegar jars can be made to order. The quality of their pottery is extremely impressive.

Excentrix Gallery & Teahouse   (097) 555 230
Bussell Highway, Cowaramup

Karen and Stan Meagher run this contemporary art gallery which specialises in experimental sculpture, pottery and art. As they are tea fanatics, it boasts the region's most amazing range of teas: from the well-known, including Earl Grey, Lapsang and Blackcurrant, to rarities such as Oolong, Chinese Green, Japanese 5 Year Branch, Yunnan and Ginseng and many more from countries such as Japan, China and South America. Coffee is also available as are light lunches and snacks.

Open daily from 10am to 5pm.

Keeping the kids occupied

THE following are ten of the Margaret River region's best attractions for kids. Most are not open on Christmas Day, Boxing Day, New Year's Day and Good Friday.

Adinfern Farm   (097) 555 272
Bussell Highway, Cowaramup

This working farm, which is situated 4 km south of Cowaramup, provides visitors with demonstrations and (in season) hands-on activities, such as bottle-feeding lambs, bucket-feeding calves, hand-feeding other animals, sheep shearing and fleece preparation.

Open daily from 11am to 5pm during school holidays and from Fridays to Sunday at all other times. Cost $3 per person.

Bannamah Wildlife Park   (097) 553 047
Caves Road, Dunsborough

Situated two kilometres west of Dunsborough on 8 hectares of natural bush and lakes, Bannamah has the region's largest range of wildlife including crocodiles, snakes, emus and dingos as well as a wide range of flora and fauna. It's possible to feed the kangaroos at any time. The Park's facilities include a cafe, kiosk, gallery and souvenir shop as well as barbecue and picnic areas.

Open daily from 9am to 5pm. Cost: $6 adults, $5 pensioners, $4 students, $3 children 2 to 12 years.

Bellview Shell Museum   (097) 576 342
Bussell Highway, Witchcliffe

Situated 8 kilometres south of Margaret River, this museum houses the largest private collection of shells from Australia and around the world. Shells may be bought, sold or exchanged and shell jewellery is for sale.

Open daily from 9am to 5pm. Cost: $4 adults, $2 children.

The Caves

The Jewel, Lake, Mammoth, Moondyne and Yallingup Caves, which were formed in limestone more than two million years ago, are spectacular and are a highlight of a trip to the region for many people. All (except the Moondyne Adventure Cave) have safely railed steps and paths.

For advanced group tour bookings, contact the Cave Supervisor (097) 584 541. All caves are closed on Christmas Day.

The Jewel Cave   (097) 584 541
Caves Road, Augusta

This is the biggest tourist cave in the state and is situated 37 kilometres south of Margaret River. No tourist cave in the world has a longer straw stalactite; 5.9 metres long and probably more than 6,000 years old. Other formations include the Frozen Waterfall, the Karri Forest and Organ Pipes Cavern. A fossil of the Tasmanian Tiger, carbon dated to be 25,000 years old, has also been discovered there. Modern lighting highlights the huge entrance chamber and key features of this magnificent cave.

Tours are conducted daily and take approximately one hour. School holidays and long weekends – 9.30am, 11 am, 12.30pm, 2pm, 3.30pm. All other times – 9.30am, 11.30am, 1.30pm, 3.30pm.

Enquiries and tickets: Cave Tour Guides Office, next to Jewel Cave Kiosk. Cost: $7.50 adults, $3.00 children.

Eagles Heritage   (097) 572 960

Boodjidup Road, Margaret River

Australia's largest collection of birds of prey: eagles, hawks, falcons and owls can be seen in a natural bush setting. The Heritage runs an endangered species breeding program and a rehabilitation centre. There are flying displays by the birds which have been trained using some aspects of the ancient art of falconry and opportunities for you to be photographed holding a hawk on your arm, with a leather gauntlet.

Open daily from 10am to 5pm. Admission: adults $4.50, children $2.50.

Ellensbrook Homestead

Off Caves Road, Margaret River

The original homestead of the pioneering Bussell family has an attractive coastal setting within a short (2km circuit) signposted, handicap accessed walk of the Meekadarabee Waterfall and is an ideal picnic spot.

Entrance fee to visit the house $2 for adults, 50c for children. Proceeds to the National Trust.

Open from 10am to 3pm daily during school holidays and from Fridays to Sundays at other times. Closed June - August.

Leeuwin Lighthouse   (097) 581 920

Leeuwin Road, Augusta

The lighthouse, which stands on the south-western tip of Australia nine kilometres south of Augusta (and 49km from Margaret River), was opened in 1896. As the tower stretches 56 metres above the mean tide level, it makes an excellent vantage point for viewing the Indian and Southern Oceans.

Open daily from 9am to 4pm. Cost of admission: $3.50 adults, $1.50 children (up to 14).

Rotary Park

Bussell Highway, Margaret River

Situated at the northern entrance to the township, this great picnic spot features barbecues, the train 'Old Kate' and relics of the timber era. The Margaret River Heritage Trail provides a pleasant walk through the karri forest and around the river.

Simmo's Ice-Creamery (097) 553 745

Commonage Road, Dunsborough

Situated just 4 kilometres from Dunsborough, Simmo's make outstanding ice-cream from local milk and cream without using artificial flavourings. There are more than twenty flavours of ice cream, freshly baked waffles and pancakes for sale. As well as this, children can view the pet deer, goats, kangaroos, emus and calves or use the playground or maze, play goofy golf or go for a hay ride. A barbecue area is also available.

Open daily in summer and all school holidays from 10.30am to 5pm: from Thursdays to Mondays in June, July, August.

Ten Mile Brook Cycle or Walk Trail

This 15 kilometre return trail takes you from the train 'Old Kate' at Rotary Park near the northern entrance to Margaret River to the Ten Mile Brook Dam which supplies water to the town. The trail winds through karri forest following the path of old railway formations to a picnic site below the dam. Toilets, seats and free barbecues are available within the Bluegum Arboretum. Disabled access. A free brochure and map is available from the Margaret River Tourist Bureau.

Winery Events

Abbey Vale Concert

Held on the last weekend in February and coinciding with the Margaret River Wine and Food Festival in conjunction with the Festival of Perth, the first Abbey Vale Concert featured the Budapest Symphony Orchestra and included arias from works by Verdi, Puccini and Lehar sung by the soprano, Katalin Szendrenyi. This alfresco concert took place in the natural amphitheatre on the banks of the spectacular lake at Abbey Vale, with a purpose built platform and shell at water's edge housing the orchestra.

The second concert featured the Odessa Philharmonic Orchestra and tickets were $80 which included reserve seating.

Enquiries: Carmel Gerrans at the vineyard (097) 552 277.

Cape Mentelle Cabernet Tasting

This tasting has become one of the major events in the Western Australian wine calendar and has been held at the Cape Mentelle Winery annually since 1982 on the last Saturday in November. In recent years, it has also been held mid-year in either Sydney or Melbourne.

Twenty 4-year-old cabernets from around the world are presented to a group of about one hundred enthusiasts. Typically, there are four Margaret River cabernets, six to eight from other parts of Australia, four from Bordeaux, four from California and, in more recent times, two from Italy. This is not a competitive tasting but an opportunity to taste a range of the world's best cabernets from the one vintage.

The wines are presented blind and their identities only revealed after all have been tasted. They are served in three brackets and the tasting is conducted in silence.

For those not experienced in tasting such a large number of wines, it can be a demanding though rewarding experience.

Certainly, it is a unique opportunity to compare cabernets from different areas without being prejudiced by knowing their cost or their origin. It also provides an opportunity for judging Margaret River reds against benchmark wines from around the world.

The tasting is followed by a relaxed lunch on the lawns of the winery. Cape Mentelle are most generous hosts and all of the wines from the tasting, a selection of current releases from Cape Mentelle, some beer and the sparkling wine of Cloudy Bay, Pelorus, can be sampled with great food.

Cost is approximately $125.

Details: Sue Juniper at the winery on (097) 573 266.

Cullen Chardonnay Tasting

Since 1985 this tasting has been on the fourth Saturday of each October. Twenty 4 year old chardonnays are presented in brackets of five. These include wines from France (Burgundy and Chablis), California, other Australian states and Margaret River and may include countries such as South Africa and New Zealand. The tasting usually includes great and expensive wines such as a Bâtard Montrachet and a Le Montrachet.

The tasting operates along similar lines to the Cape Mentelle Cabernet Tasting with the wines being presented masked, in brackets of five, in silence. The identity of the chardonnays is only revealed after all have been tasted. Unlike at Cape Mentelle, the scores of those tasting are added up and the results of the preferences of the consumers and the trade are circulated afterwards.

Lunch is accompanied by current releases from Cullen. Cost approximately $100.

Enquiries: Di Cullen (097) 555 277

Leeuwin Estate Concert

After a decade of success, the annual Leeuwin Concert is one of Western Australia's great social occasions. Held in the open air on the lawns of the winery against a backdrop of huge karri trees, the concert has featured the London Philharmonic, the Berlin State Orchestra, Ray Charles, Kiri Te Kanawa and James Galway, Tom Jones, Dionne Warwick, Diana Ross, and George Benson pitted against the famous Leeuwin kookaburras. The concert is held in February or March and is usually sold out immediately tickets go on sale. Cost approximately $80.

Enquiries: Leeuwin Estate (09) 430 4099.

Margaret River Wine and Food Festival

This festival is held on the last weekend in February and features the open air concert at the Abbey Vale Vineyard, a Friday night street dance in Margaret River, a Saturday morning hogshead handicap and a major Saturday afternoon tasting of the wines of the region held at Pioneer Park in Cowaramup. A highlight is a gourmet lunch on Sunday at Leeuwin Estate which in the past has featured top Australian chefs, Phillip Searle, Greg Brown and Stephanie Alexander, local produce and a vast range of Margaret River wines. The area's restaurants put on special menus for the Saturday evening.

Enquiries: Margaret River Tourist Bureau (097) 573 476.

Prelude to Vintage Tasting

This is the major promotion in Perth of the Margaret River Wine Industry Association. Held in early February at one of Perth's five star hotels, it features the new release wines from more than 30 Margaret River wineries. Each producer sets up a stall and offers tastings of its available wines between 3 and 8pm. Entry costs $10, if booked, or $15 at the door. Tickets are available from the wineries and some fine wine stores in Perth.

Enquiries: Sue Bussau (097) 581 903.

The Willyabrup Descent

Held on the weekend following the Perth Wine Show (usually the second in September), this is a race in which teams representing the different wineries of the region attempt to steer their wine barrel down the Willyabrup Brook from Ribbon Vale to Pierro. Which is more preposterous, the fancy dress of the competitors or their antics in attempting to gain unfair advantage over their opponents, is often a mute point. Whatever the result, the day is dedicated to fun, cheating and camaraderie within the wine industry.

Enquiries: Mike Davies (097) 556 271.

The Willyabrup Spring Celebration

This celebration of wine, food and art is held each year on the October long weekend. In 1994, fifteen wineries of the Willyabrup Valley joined together for the spring festival. Each of the wineries involved featured the work of one or more significant local artist. These included the wood crafts of Greg Collins at Brookland Valley, the wrought iron works of Malcolm Paine at Woody Nook, clay jewellery by Debbie Beckett at Sandalford, mixed media works by Trish Durham at Willespie, hand blown glass by Peter Moorfoot at Pierro and watercolours and oils by Raymond Barnes at Arlewood.

The festivities always provides a great opportunity to visit this sub-region of the Margaret River, to meet winemakers and artists and to sample the spring releases.

Enquiries: Allison Kelly (097) 556 285.

Accommodation in the region

The Augusta Margaret River Tourist Bureau provides a free booking service for accommodation in the region seven days a week on (097) 572 911. The following are some of the best examples of the accommodation available in the area in a range of different categories.

Hotels and Motels

Caves House   (097) 552 131
Caves Road, Yallingup

The hotel dates back to 1903, although the gracious main building was constructed after a fire in 1939. Set in beautifully landscaped grounds with ocean views; 43 rooms, some with en-suite, tv, fans, electric blankets, laundry, fridge, guest lounge, games room, tennis courts, bowling and croquet lawns. Percolated coffee available in the lounge. Horse and bicycling riding can be arranged. From $65 to $225 double.

Colonial Motel   (097) 572 633
Wallcliffe Road, Margaret River

Set in native and landscaped grounds, twenty modern units with en-suites, some with cooking facilities, fans, electric blankets, heaters, tv, videos, fridge, laundry, communal kitchen, pool, tennis court. From $59 - $85 double.

Margaret River Hotel   (097) 572 655
Bussell Highway, Margaret River

Set in the main street, old building with 27 rooms, some with en-suites, heaters, tv. From $75 - $150 double.

Quality Captain Freycinet (097) 572 033

Bussell Highway, Margaret River

Modern motel on corner of Tunbridge Street, recently upgraded, back from the main street and quiet; 62 airconditioned rooms with en-suites, tv, videos, mini bar, coffee shop with percolated coffee, room service, restaurant, fridge, laundry, pool, children's playground. From $96 - $115 double.

Bed and Breakfast

The Merchants (097) 572 157

Lot 1, Ashton Street, Margaret River

Situated on 60 acres, overlooking the Margaret River; 2 double rooms with queen sized beds and en-suites, log fire in winter, percolated coffee in the lounge, laundry, heated pool. $80 double.

Old Bakehouse (097) 555 462

Bussell Highway, Cowaramup

Four rooms, one with en-suite, three with shared facilities, electric blankets, in 1930's home. Percolated coffee during day. Evening meals on request. $55 - $80 double.

Sandyknowe (097) 555 336

Miamup Road, Cowaramup

Situated just 3 km from Cowaramup, this is a farmstay where you can share in some farm activities such as milking. Private entrance. Three rooms with queen sized beds and en-suites, one family unit with en-suite, two doubles or twins with shared facilities. Electric blankets, pots of tea and percolated coffee. From $60 - $70 double, $5 -$20 child.

Wallcliffe Lodge   (097) 572 699
Wilderness Road, Margaret River

Six kms from town in bush surrounds, overlooking a national park; en-suite or shared facilities, tv, electric blankets, heaters, guest lounge with fire in winter. Percolated coffee. No smoking except on the balcony. No pets. Evening meals available except on Wednesday and Saturday. From $60 to $80 double.

Lodges

Yungarra Lodge   (097) 552 153
Yungarra Drive, Dunsborough

Five chalets with sweeping views of Geographe Bay, each of which can accommodate four (double, 2 single beds), breakfast available, log fires, microwave, barbecue, electric blankets. Breakfast available in chalets. From $85 double plus $29.50 per person.

Guest Houses
(rates include breakfast)

Basildene Homestead   (097) 573 140
Wallcliffe Road, Margaret River

Classified by the National Trust, this 1912 building has 10 individually decorated rooms with en-suites (8 with queen sized beds, 2 with twins), one of which is suitable for disabled persons, electric blankets, central heating, evening meals available. From $115 - $135 double.

Cape Lodge   (097) 556 311
Caves Road, Yallingup

Situated between Abbey Farm and Johnson Roads, this impressive, recently-built, Cape Dutch mansion is set amid 16 hectares of jarrah forest and protea plantings with lawns, rose garden and a lake; 11 luxurious rooms with en-suites, 3 queen sized beds, 8 king sized beds, 3 with spas, electric blankets, air conditioning, hairdryers, iron and board, minibar, large, elegant guest lounge with filter coffee during the day and log fire in winter, tv, outstanding breakfasts. A favourite of mine. From $115 - $190 double.

Gilgara Homestead   (097) 572 705
Caves Road, Willyabrup

Situated near the corner with Carter Road, this large modern house has been built in the style of the 1870s; 6 rooms with en-suites, fans, heaters, electric blankets, queen sized beds, coffee plungers, pots of tea in lounge available at all times, fresh cakes daily, lounge, open fire in winter, home cooking available. From $120 - $140 double.

Margaret River Guesthouse   (097) 572 349
Valley Road, Margaret River

Formerly an Anglican convent, built in 1928, and set in a quiet cul-de-sac close to the township with attractive gardens; 3 rooms with en-suites, fans, heaters, fridge, 5 rooms with shared facilities, electric blankets, central lounge. From $60 to $80 double.

The Noble Grape   (097) 555 538
Bussell Highway, Cowaramup

Comfortable, new, purpose-built guest house furnished with antiques; 6 rooms with en-suites including a family suite of two rooms which can accommodate 6, heaters, bar fridge, tv, great breakfasts, dinners by request. From $70 to $80 double.

Chalets

Burnside Bungalows   (097) 572 139
291A Burnside Road, Margaret River

Two limestone chalets in a peaceful, private setting 5 minutes from Margaret River; fully self-contained, bath, doonas & pillows, linen hire, tv, wood fires, washing machine, iron, barbecue, mountain bikes for hire. From $60 (mid-week) to $70 (weekend) double, $5 per extra person.

Karridale Cottages   (097) 585 598
Karridale

About 33 km south of Margaret River; 4 stone and earth cottages set amidst 20 hectares of natural bush; 2 single roomed (1 double bed and 1 sofa) and 2 double roomed cottages (1 double bed plus two bunks, to sleep a total of six) all with en-suites, self-contained, log fire, doonas and pillows, linen hire, games room with table tennis, communal laundry. From $50-$70 double, $5 per extra person.

Margaret River Chalets   (097) 572 905
Bussell Highway, Margaret River

Just 2 km south of the township through the old railway reserve; 3 cottages, sleeping up to 6, modern furnishings, self-contained, tv, pot belly heating, microwave, washing machine, gas barbecue. Linen for hire. No pets. From $60 double.

Timber Creek Cottages   (097) 556 254
Willyabrup

Three timber cottages similar to those of group settlement houses in secluded bushland settings one in Yelverton and two in Carter Road, Willyabrup. Two cottages accommodate eight: 1 double bed and 1 bunk in each of two rooms. One cottage with one double bed and one single in open plan room. Self-contained, toilets, showers, baths, tvs, washing machine in one, irons, blankets & pillows, linen hire. Double from $55 (midweek) -$75 for weekends. $350-$500 weekly.

Caravan Parks

Canal Rocks Caravan Park   (097) 552 116
Yallingup

Situated on the beachfront, 55 powered and 20 unpowered sites; showers, toilets, recreation room, playground, laundry, barbecues, tennis and volleyball courts, shop and restaurants.

Prevelly Park Resort   (097) 572 374
Prevelly Park

Well-shaded park close to the beach with 90 sites, 50 of which are powered; barbecues, kiosk, ice available, liquor store on site. 20 on-site vans to accommodate four to six, blankets, linen and pillows required. Three cottages to accommodate six in three bedrooms; two cottages to accommodate four; shower, fridge, cooking facilities, heaters available, linen hire. No dogs.

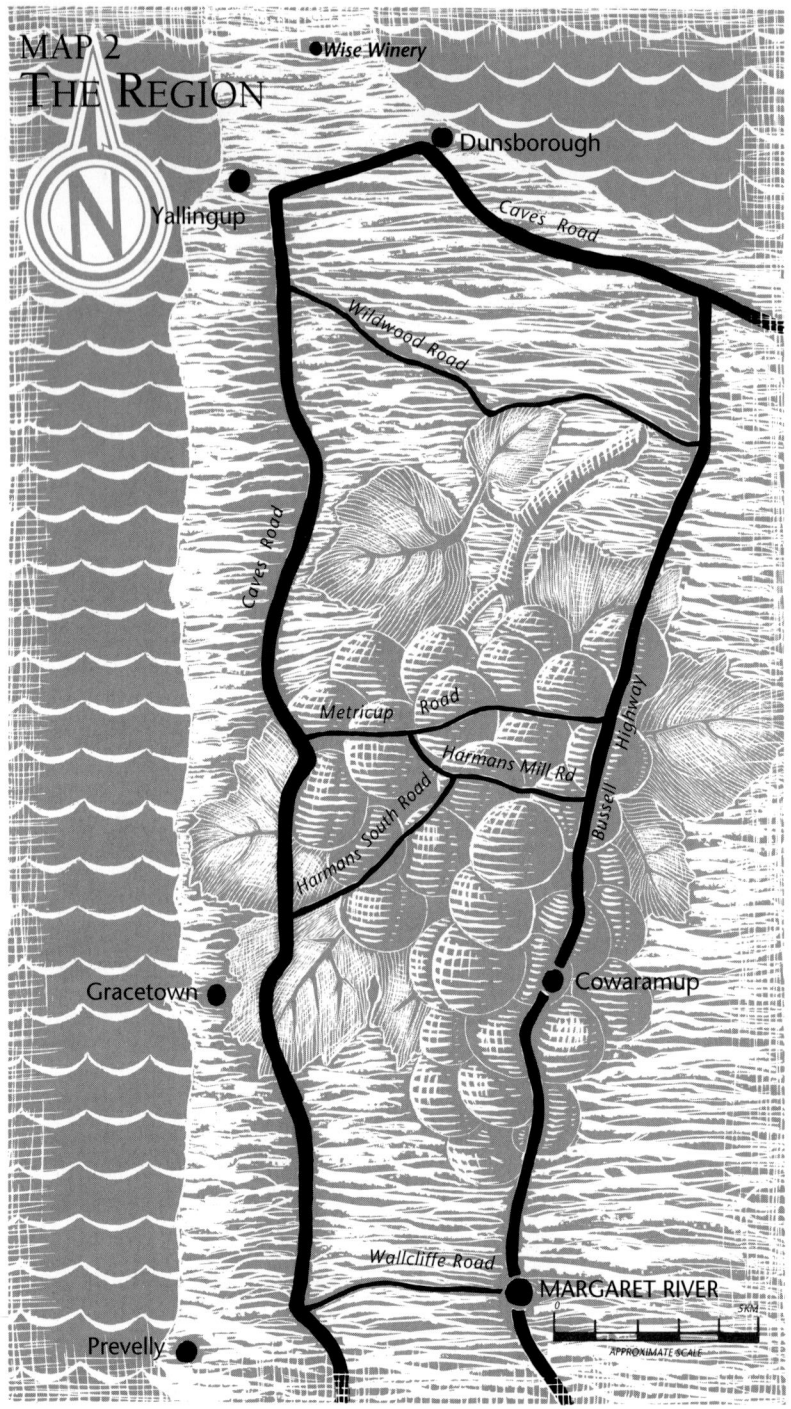

MAP 2
THE REGION

Wise Winery

Dunsborough

Yallingup

Caves Road

Wildwood Road

Caves Road

Metricup Road

Harmans Mill Rd

Bussell Highway

Harmans South Road

Gracetown

Cowaramup

Wallcliffe Road

MARGARET RIVER

Prevelly

APPROXIMATE SCALE

0   5KM

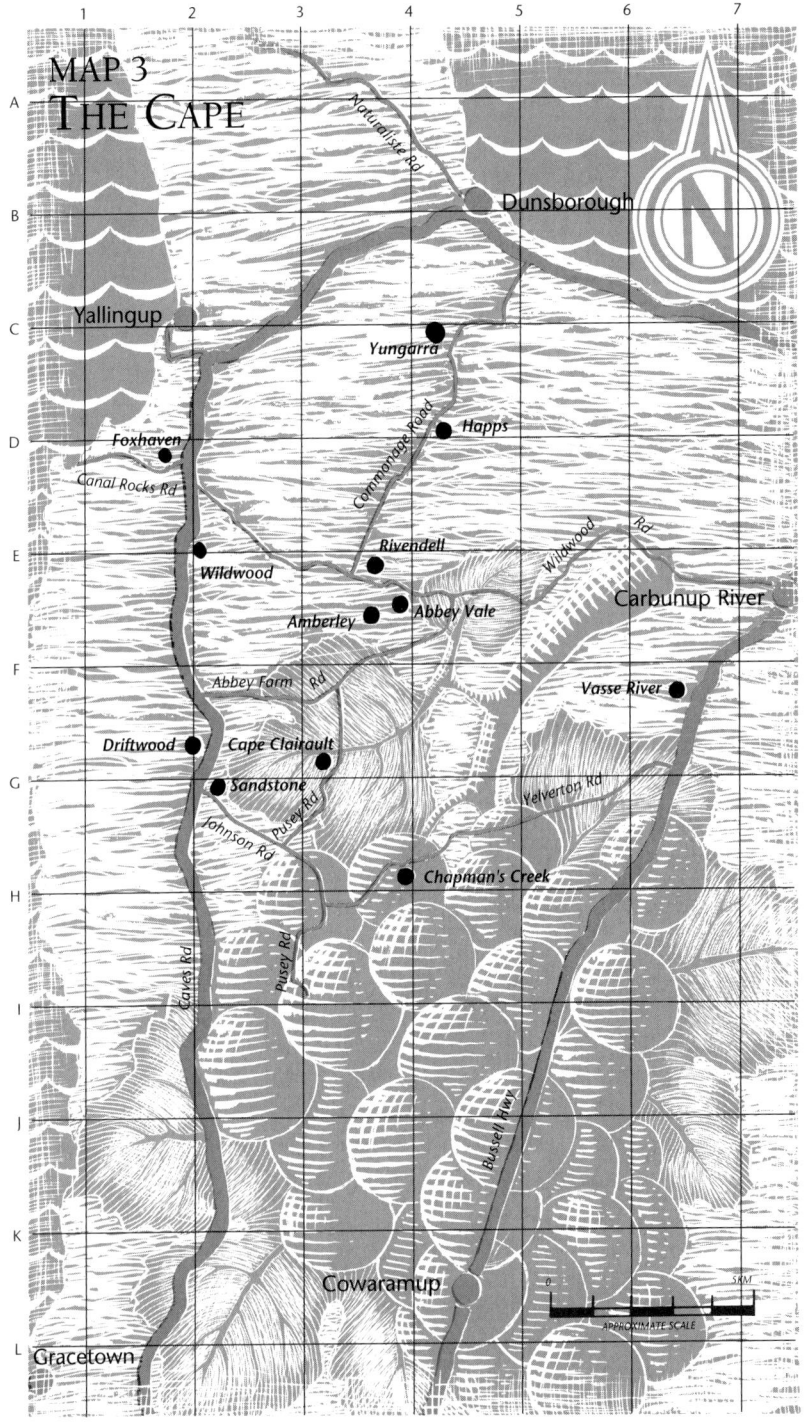

MAP 3
THE CAPE

Naturaliste Rd

Dunsborough

Yallingup

Yungarra

Happs

Foxhaven

Canal Rocks Rd

Commonage Road

Rivendell

Wildwood

Wildwood Rd

Amberley

Abbey Vale

Carbunup River

Abbey Farm Rd

Vasse River

Driftwood

Cape Clairault

Sandstone

Pusey Rd

Velverton Rd

Johnson Rd

Chapman's Creek

Caves Rd

Pusey Rd

Bussell Hwy

Cowaramup

0   5KM

APPROXIMATE SCALE

Gracetown

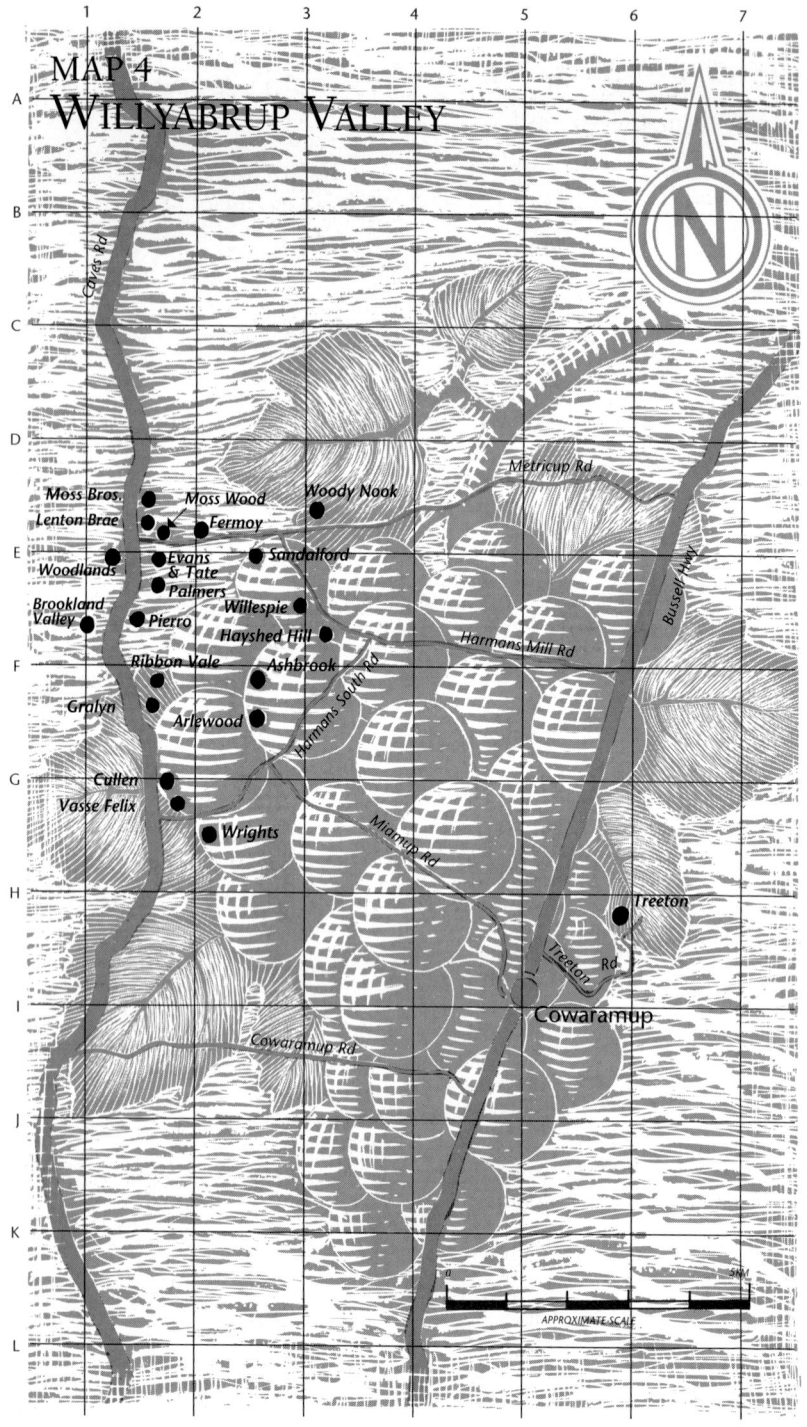

MAP 4
WILLYABRUP VALLEY

Caves Rd

Metricup Rd

Bussell Hwy

Moss Bros.
Lenton Brae
Moss Wood
Fermoy
Woody Nook

Woodlands
Evans
& Tate
Palmers
Sandalford

Brookland
Valley
Pierro
Willespie
Hayshed Hill

Harmans Mill Rd

Ribbon Vale
Ashbrook

Harmans South Rd

Gralyn
Arlewood

Cullen
Vasse Felix
Wrights

Midmup Rd

Treeton

Treeton Rd

Cowaramup

Cowaramup Rd

APPROXIMATE SCALE

154

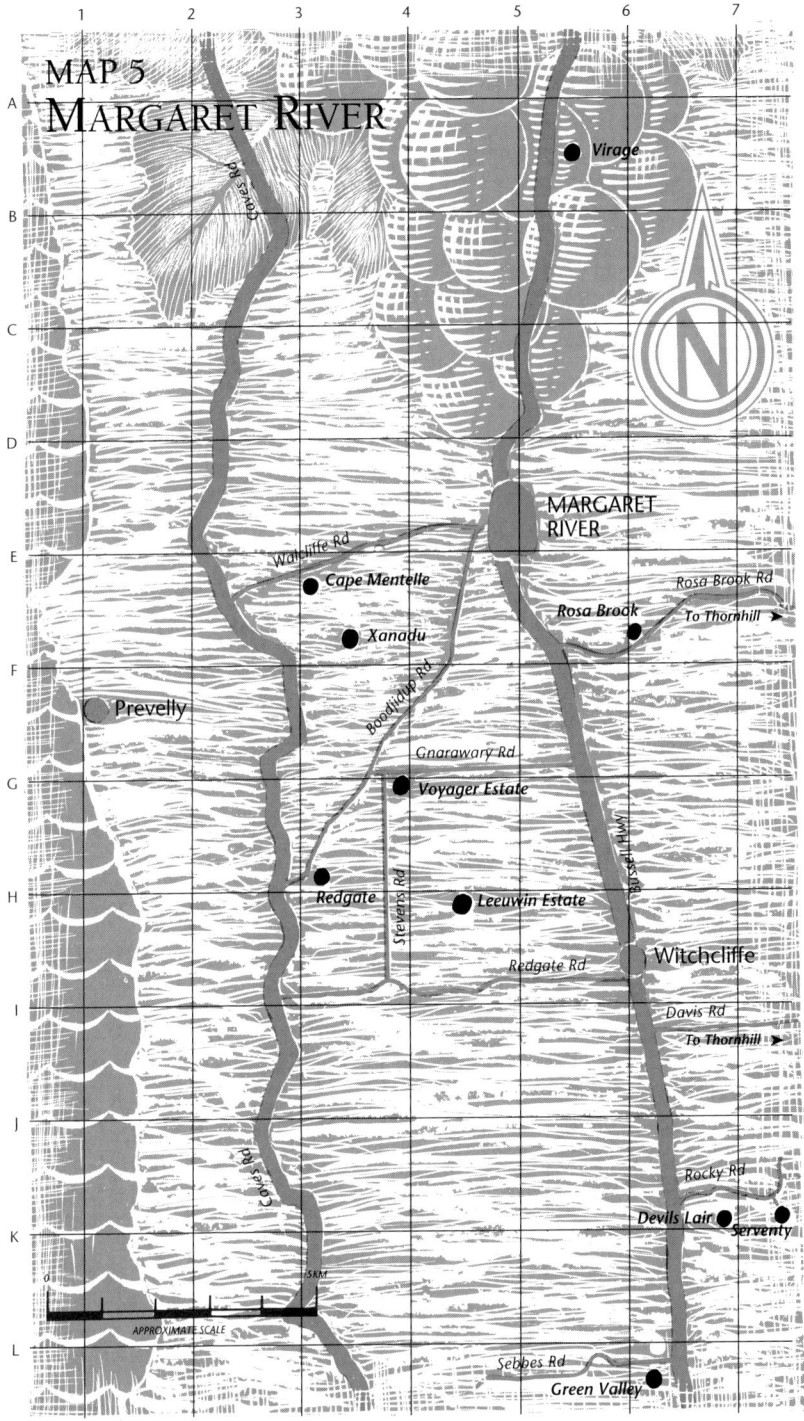

MAP 5
MARGARET RIVER

1 2 3 4 5 6 7

A

Virage

B

C

N

D

MARGARET
RIVER

E

Wallcliffe Rd

Cape Mentelle

Rosa Brook Rd

Rosa Brook

To Thornhill ➤

Xanadu

F

Boodjidup Rd

Prevelly

Gnarawary Rd

G

Voyager Estate

Stevens Rd

H

Redgate

Leeuwin Estate

Witchcliffe

Redgate Rd

I

Davis Rd

To Thornhill ➤

J

Caves Rd

Rocky Rd

K

Devils Lair

Seventy

0   5KM

APPROXIMATE SCALE

L

Sebbes Rd

Green Valley

Russell Hwy

Caves Rd

Index

Wine notes

Wine notes

Wine notes